RESEARCH HIGHLIGHTS IN SOCIAL WORK 27

Planning and Costing Community Care

Edited by Chris Clark and Irvine Lapsley

Jessica Kingsley Publishers
London and Bristol, Pennsylvania

Robert Gordon University
School of Applied Social Science
Kepplestone Annexe, Queen's Road
Aberdeen AB9 2PG

First published in the United Kingdom in 1996 by
Jessica Kingsley Publishers Ltd
116 Pentonville Road
London N1 9JB, England
and
1900 Frost Road, Suite 101
Bristol, PA 19007, U S A

Copyright © 1996 Robert Gordon University,
Research Highlights Advisory Group, School of Applied Social Science

Library of Congress Cataloging in Publication Data
A CIP catalogue record for this book is available from the Library of Congress

British Library Cataloguing in Publication Data
A CIP catalogue record for this book is available from the British Library

ISBN 1 85302 267 5

Printed and Bound in Great Britian by
Cromwell Press, Melksham, Wiltshire

Contents

Introduction

Chris Clark and Irvine Lapsley

The aim of this book is to examine some of the issues that the new policy regime in community care raises for service practitioners and managers. Under the concept of care or case management which has been adopted as a cornerstone of community care, two processes are fundamental. They are the assessment of individuals' need for services in the community, and the planning and costing of services to meet their needs (Department of Health 1991a, b). The focus in the chapters which follow is on planning for individual recipients of community care, and on the service and management structures which deliver individual care planning. The separate task of preparing global care plans for a local area, which also figures in the new responsibilities of the local authorities, is not addressed in this book except in passing.

The contributions to this book therefore embrace both policy and practice issues. These extend beyond the conventional domain of social care management to include consideration of costs and budgeting as essential ingredients of this new regime. The key issues addressed in the implementation of care management in service delivery practice, and costing and budgeting considerations, are briefly outlined here.

The implementation of care management in practice

Several chapters in this volume focus on the implementation of care management since 1993. Alison Petch records research amongst Scottish local authorities on their patchy and extremely variable adoption of new methods and systems intended to implement the new national policy. Laura Bannerman and Bill Robertson offer a first-hand description of the process within one local authority. Terry McLean concentrates on the assessment tools and methods which are crucial to effective care management practice. Their accounts very clearly demonstrate that implementing care management is a massive and complex undertaking surrounded by huge uncertainties. It is far from the rationalistic application of plain truths and commonsense that the bullet-point language of official guidance so persistently but misleadingly presents. In their survey of voluntary sector responses, Stephen Maxwell and Mike Titterton similarly show that the expectations of both voluntary organisations and local authorities of a new contract culture have not corresponded with the reality. Phyllis Sturges rounds out the picture by comparing current British experience with the longer and more varied experience of the USA. This comparison undermines optimism about the soundness of some of the current British effort.

Costing and budgets in community care

A central theme of the new care management is that it will be facilitated by the devolution of budgets. Irvine Lapsley explores the subtlety of budget-setting in the private sector context and points to the difficulties of transplanting such mechanisms to public sector environments. Whether arrived at by accident or design, the current, relatively slow and uneven adoption of devolved budgets and unit costing within the complex area of social care is to be welcomed. The tensions between these new financial disciplines and the values embedded within social care make rapid implementation difficult.

The need for more refined cost estimation is demonstrated by the chapter on care management by Lorna Cameron and Isobel Freeman. This underlines the complexity of specific cases confronting care managers within one local authority. It also shows the indirect and limited manner in which costing information impinges on such activities; for example, most packages of care tend not to be formally costed.

However, it should not be thought that there has been no progress within this area of constructing new, refined costing information. Two contributions describe pioneering work. These studies differ in their focus and settings, but offer approaches to costing which extend beyond the conventional and afford the possibility of meaningful connections between the world of financial discipline and the decision processes of social workers. Margaret King and Sue Llewellyn describe the costs and quality of care of disabled people in a case study setting. This reveals a potentially novel means of constructing costs, and a cost classification scheme which would be of benefit to both management of care provider facilities and the purchasers of social care in their contract-setting arrangements. Anne Netten's study extends beyond the boundaries of a specific residential facility to consider the constituent elements of care costs in community care settings. The chapter examines the thorny problem of informal care costs, which poses a challenging task for care managers and finance experts in local authorities. Difficulties are accentuated by the unclear relationships of the many agencies – health boards, local government, and possibly private and voluntary operators – in the field of care.

In conclusion, the contributions to this book explore some of the dilemmas created for practitioners and agencies by the unavoidable predicament of having to cost and compare what may well be regarded as incommensurable. They cannot offer simple solutions, but they enlarge our understanding of the problems on the basis of research and practical experience. Caring is a complex idea, and the argument of this book is that care management has to address a range of issues that are much more than merely technical. It is hoped that policy makers, managers, social workers, finance staff and researchers will find this book helpful as they seek to refine the implementation of community care.

References

Department of Health, Social Services Inspectorate and Scottish Office, Social Work Services Group (1991a) *Care Management and Assessment: Managers' Guide*. London: HMSO.

Department of Health, Social Services Inspectorate and Scottish Office, Social Work Services Group (1991b) *Care Management and Assessment: Practitioners' Guide*. London: HMSO.

Chapter 1

Care Management
Putting the Principles into Practice

Alison Petch

Twelve months after the release of the April 1993 trigger, we can start to appraise the reality of care management in practice. Early experience in the US had hinted at an agenda (Beardshaw and Towell 1990, Huxley 1993). Demonstration projects in the UK had revealed what could be managed under particular and privileged circumstances (Challis and Davies 1986, Challis *et al.* 1988, Challis *et al.* 1989, Cambridge 1992). Issues particular to specific care groups had been explored (Dant and Gearing 1990, Pilling 1992, Onyett 1992). The plethora of guidance and associated training had set the blueprint (Department of Health 1990, Department of Health 1991a, b). Individual authorities had pursued their own pilot projects (Richardson and Higgins 1990, Meethan, Thompson and Parker 1993, Petch, Stalker, Taylor and Taylor 1994, Cameron and Freeman in this volume). Only when care management becomes routine, however, can its effectiveness as a core methodology for identifying and responding to individual need begin to be assessed.

Policy guidance

A number of familiar themes tend to recur throughout the debates on care management. Foremost amongst them are whether core tasks are undertaken by a single worker or by several, and whether the worker(s) operate within a single or multiple agency setting. In addition, the care manager may be integrated or separate from the key agency, and may have limited or extensive budgetary control.

A further organisational distinction common in the literature is between what has been termed the 'administrative' and the 'complete' or, in the context particularly of mental health provision, the 'clinical' model (Huxley 1993). In the latter the care manager is involved in the provision of aspects of care; in the former service arrangement and coordination are seen as the core tasks.

The guidance on care management from the Department of Health and the Scottish Office (Department of Health 1991a, b) identified a number of organisational models. At single agency level, five are detailed, including the administrative model but also, for example, the user acting as his or her own care manager and a shared tasks model whereby core tasks are shared by a combination of professionally and vocationally qualified staff. A further five models are discussed for the operation of care management on an inter-agency basis, with variations in the form of lead, joint, multi and independent agency roles. Advantages and disadvantages are posited for each of the models, whilst recognising that most of the developments up to that point in this country had tended to the single care manager model, with varying degrees of budgetary responsibility.

Emergent models

As part of their investigation into Efficiency and Effectiveness in the Delivery of Community Care, a project funded by the Scottish Office, the Social Work Research Centre at the University of Stirling explored the initial approaches to care management being adopted by local authorities in Scotland. Key informants from agencies were interviewed on two occasions, the first at the end of 1992 and the second in the summer of 1993 (Buglass 1993, Stalker, Taylor and Petch 1994). Three provisional models were identified from the first round of interviews and confirmed at the later stage. Amongst the multitude of models explored in the literature, these were the ones actually to be found at the grass roots. They can be summarised as follows:

Model 1: care management as a separate job

Model 2: care management as a role or task within an existing job and within a single agency (the social work department)

Model 3: care management as a role or task operating within a joint health and social work structure.

The preference of each of the Scottish authorities at that stage is indicated in Table 1.1. It should be stressed, however, that certain authorities were still finalising their plans. Lothian, in particular, had designated the first twelve months as a period of pilot work and was not finalising its procedures until 1994.

Model 1: Care management as a separate job

In this model care management is viewed as a new concept, to be carried out by individuals in a separate, 'designated' post. Primacy is given to the separation of the task of assessment from the provision of services. The care manager, having discussed with the user and carer a range of service responses to the identified needs, then negotiates the care package with colleagues on the resource side. The care manager should also cost the package of care. It is argued that in order to provide a genuinely needs-led assessment the assessor must be independent of the services available, free from any compromise of assessing for services for which they may also be responsible. Separation of the tasks should also promote greater advocacy on behalf of the client.

Table 1.1: Models of Care Management

	Separate Job	*Single-agency task*	*Joint agency task*
Tayside	*		
Grampian	*		
Lothian		*	
Strathclyde		*	
Borders		*	
Central		*	
Fife		*	
Highland		*	
Shetland			*
Orkney			*
Western Isles			*
Dumfries & Galloway			*

This model has been adopted in the first instance by Grampian and Tayside, influenced in large part by experience in their own pilot projects (Taylor, Scott and Rowley 1993, Petch *et al.* 1994). Those performing care management do so exclusively and are based in care management teams. Referrals are initially screened by a Senior Care Manager and those which appear indicative of complex needs are allocated to a care manager. He or she will then pursue the key tasks of assessment, care planning, implementation of the care plan, monitoring and review. The process is seen as one of 'inter-linking care tasks which should not be viewed as separate activities but as part of a unified whole' (Grampian Regional Council 1993:4). Once the package appears well established, staff on the provider side will take over responsibility for day-to-day monitoring. Reference should be made back to the care manager for any adjustment other than minor to the care package, with the care manager retaining responsibility for formal reviews.

Model 2: Care management as a task within a single agency
The majority of regions currently operate this model, in which individuals adopt the role of care manager as appropriate alongside their other tasks. There are no separate teams and no individuals with specific designations. For certain of the regions this was a well thought out position; for others it might be regarded as the default option, possibly subject to change after early experimentation. Highland, for example, hopes to move towards care management according to Model 1 in the future.

Several of those interviewed at the initial stage were somewhat apologetic about their adoption of this model, aware of the divergence from government guidelines. There was agreement with the analysis of the problems care management was intended to address, in particular the fragmentation of services and the need for greater user and carer participation, but informants were not fully convinced that the separation of purchasing and service provision at field level was the correct solution. They considered that coordination of care was the crucial dimension for providing clients with an improved service, and believed that this could be achieved without the creation of a separate care manager post. Indeed in Strathclyde and Lothian, reference is to care coordination and care management is not an accepted term. Borders argued that their rural nature would create particular problems if a model requiring separate posts were to be adopted.

A key question in relation to this model must be the extent to which assessment can be kept separate from service delivery. While acting as care manager for a particular client, the same individual should not, in theory, also deliver a social work service to that person. Various factors, however, may conspire against the care managers' ability to keep their different roles entirely separate – shortage of resources, slow progress in developing a mixed economy of care, sheer expediency. An evaluation of a pilot project operating this model found care managers providing a variety of direct services to users, including occupational therapy, counselling, and practical assistance with budgeting and shopping (Petch *et al.* 1994).

Model 3: Care management as a joint task within local authority and health board
The joint agency model is being adopted in four regions. Care management is again a task undertaken when appropriate within the framework of an existing job, but under this model it is perceived as a joint responsibility shared between agencies. Some mechanism linking the local authority and health board is therefore built into the structure, a multidisciplinary team or some regular meeting. Decisions are then taken as to the most appropriate individual to be the care manager for each case.

The Primary Assessment Teams (PATs) in Dumfries and Galloway are the best established example of this model, although again the term care manager has been strongly rejected in favour of care coordinator, following representations from health professionals. Weekly meetings between members of local adult care teams and primary health care teams consider referrals of older and physically disabled people with 'complex' needs (meaning in this instance a mixture of health and social care needs). A care coordinator is appointed to lead the assessment and to carry out other care coordination tasks. The local authority retains control of financial arrangements, but the care coordinator can be from either agency. If, however, a residential or nursing home placement is part of an individual's package, a social worker, if not already involved, will take on responsibility for monitoring and review. The activities of the PATs are mirrored, in respect of people with learning difficulties, by community learning disability teams.

A not dissimilar arrangement operates in the Western Isles, where members of local social work teams meet every three weeks with colleagues from primary care to form community care teams. A typical team will comprise the GP, a social worker, a home care organiser and two district nurses. Members of the team both provide a service according to their professional training, and are responsible for purchasing other services. In all three of the island communities, however, respondents at the second interview from the local authority perceived more joint working than the health boards.

In England a similar fundamental division is to be found between authorities who have interpreted care management as a process, its component activities undertaken by a range of individuals, and those who have seen it as a function of a particular post. In a sample of 33 authorities (JICC 1993), departments were roughly evenly divided on this dimension. Overall, however, the dominant impression was of

> 'the complexity and confusion of the national scene arising from the different ways in which care management has been interpreted in different authorities.' (p.4)

Professional background of care managers or coordinators

Local authorities have been encouraged to draw from a range of agencies and professions when appointing care managers, key attributes, for example 'good interpersonal skills and imagination' (Audit Commission 1992), not being the province of any single group. Agencies were asked who in principle they would consider eligible to act as a care manager. Social workers, not surprisingly, are universally eligible. In virtually all areas, occupational therapists can also act as care managers, and in most this is common practice. At the interview stage only two regions specifically identified home care organisers as potential care managers, and in Strathclyde only in relation to relatively straightforward cases. In other areas, home care organisers may be part of a community care team but do not adopt a care manager role; elsewhere, they lead a home care team alongside the community care team but are not considered members of the latter. A common response was that home care organisers are potentially well qualified for the care management role in that they are accustomed to managing complex coordination of resources, but may require some enhanced training.

The majority of regions saw members of primary health care teams as potential care managers. In most cases, however, this was a hypothetical position; agreements had not necessarily been reached with health boards, or if agreed had not yet been translated into procedures. In summer 1993, only in three areas were health care personnel acting as care managers: in

Dumfries and Galloway, in Strathclyde in relation to people with learning difficulties or mental health problems, and in Tayside through secondment of health board staff to the local authority.

The picture presented by health boards tended to be less clear and less optimistic as to likely developments. At the same time, most health boards approved the principle of embracing the care management role where appropriate, particularly in relation to individuals with learning difficulties or mental health problems. For the latter group, particularly, however, considerable confusion remains between the role of the keyworker defined under the care programme approach (North and Ritchie 1993, Schneider 1993) and the duties accorded to the care manager. Whatever the precise role, however, the community psychiatric nurse would appear well placed to fulfil it. In rural areas, where health board personnel are often more numerous, a particular logic was presented for them to assume care management responsibilities. In order for such possibilities to expand there would have to be a clarity on financial arrangements between the two agencies which is not yet in place.

Primary health care staff have a key role in the referral of individuals for care management. In certain areas – Lothian, Grampian, the Western Isles, Shetland and parts of Tayside – care managers are aligned to GP practices, with GPs closely involved in the assessment itself – in Dumfries and Galloway, through the PAT teams, and in the Western Isles, through Community Care Teams. Lothian, particularly strong on GP involvement, has a liaison GP appointed to each of the social work districts. Moreover a panel of GPs in each district is being set up, prepared to act as a 'flying squad' to carry out assessments if a patient's own GP does not wish to be involved.

While most authorities have not ruled out the possibility of staff from other statutory agencies taking on the care management role in respect of individual users, very few had concrete proposals at the time of interview. District housing departments are asked to contribute information to assessment where appropriate, although the extent to which this is a formalised procedure and the frequency with which it occurs varies. Further collaboration may be indicated after finalisation of the circular on community care and housing, out for consultation in draft form at the time of writing (Scottish Office 1994).

The contribution of individuals from the voluntary sector in the role of care manager is complicated by their identity as service providers. 'Service-specific' assessments are being carried out by some, for example

Crossroads Care Attendant Schemes, with the proviso that cases showing indications of more complex needs will be referred back to the local authority. A similar situation pertains in the private sector. It was generally recognised that private residential and nursing establishments should play a part in assessing whether or not they could meet the needs of a particular individual; one respondent aptly described the role as contributing to care planning, rather than to assessment.

Several authorities are now considering the issue of accreditation for care managers, including the extent to which this should be linked to professional background. As highlighted above, within the local authority the focus of particular debate may be the home care organiser; cross agency any trend towards accreditation may restrict participation in the first instance.

A more radical option is that service users and/or their carers should act as their own care managers (Smale and Tuson 1993). Early policy guidance from the Department of Health endorsed the possibility:

> 'It may be possible for some service users to play a more active part in their own care management, for example assuming responsibility for the day-to-day management of their carers may help to meet the aspirations of severely physically disabled people to be as independent as possible.' (Department of Health 1990, p.5)

Such a possibility was endorsed in principle by three-quarters of the Scottish authorities. In practice, however, it is only currently pursued in a handful of cases, including a pilot project in Lothian.

Allocation of a care manager

The semantics of care management have been unnecessarily complicated by the tendency to extract the assessment stage and to refer to it as if it were a separate process, rather than one of the seven core tasks. The danger of confusion is compounded by the potential need to distinguish, first, assessment of need from care planning, and, second, care management as a whole from service delivery.

The need to distinguish assessment of need from care planning is emphasised in official guidance (Department of Health 1991a). In terms of personnel, however, assessment is not generally separated from other care management tasks, the same person generally being responsible for both. This includes four regions where the decision to appoint a care manager is only taken following the outcome of the assessment; where a care manager is deemed appropriate the original assessor will normally be appointed. In Shetland, however, the appointed care manager may well be someone other than the initial assessor. An exception in terms of separating the tasks is found with the hospital-based care managers in Aberdeen where a social worker undertakes the assessment of need and the care manager takes over to put together a care package and prepare a care plan.

A summary can be attempted of the evolving arrangements for the appointment of a care manager. In ten regions a care manager is only appointed to individual cases following a clear decision to do so. In four, Dumfries and Galloway, Western Isles, Orkney and Shetland, the decision is made by a multidisciplinary group, while in Fife a case conference is held, and health professionals involved if appropriate. In other regions the decision is normally taken by a social work senior. In about half the regions this decision is made at the point of initial screening (but can be reversed if further assessment is contra-indicative), while in the other authorities a care manager is appointed following assessment.

The criteria for appointing a care manager vary, both in content and specificity. They relate in large part to the level of response at the assessment stage. The more complex typologies for screening and assessment outlined in the guidance have been eschewed. Most regions operate on the basis of initial screening, followed by some form of simple or more complex assessment. Tayside is unusual in identifying four different levels of assessment. These embrace 'initial' (screening), 'specific-service' (for example for occupational therapy or home help, where a care manager is not involved), 'standard' (complex needs) and 'specialist' (an additional assessment by another care professional, for example a psychologist). The process of screening is perhaps the most variable, with in some regions all referrals receiving some kind of screening, in others only those requiring assessment being formally screened. Screening was characterised by one local authority respondent as the stage of care management with 'the biggest elastic band around it'.

In certain situations a complex assessment is mandatory, for example people entering residential or nursing care, or disabled people under Section 4 of the Disabled Persons (Services, Representation and Consultation) Act 1986. Other criteria would focus on aspects of risk and vulnerability, further defined perhaps as risk of emotional or physical harm, risk of loss of independence, risk of reduced quality of life.

Translated into criteria for the appointment of a care manager, the considerations can generally be characterised as complexity of need and number of services required, although complexity of need often remains undefined. Strathclyde, avoiding rigid criteria, works to a list of features associated with complexity.

The account of care management presented by Central replicated that found in their care management pilot (Petch *et al.* 1994). Motivated by a desire to avoid a two-tier response, care management is presented as part of a 'continuum' rather than a distinct process or activity. There is no specific point at which a decision is taken that a case will be care managed, nor set criteria for its selection. Such a fluid approach to the concept does, however, raise other issues in relation to equity.

Devolved budgets

The decentralised budget was key to several of the original pilot projects evaluated by PSSRU (Challis and Davies 1986). Frontline practitioners had direct control of a certain amount of money with which to develop a range of responses to individual needs. Subsequently the devolution of budgetary responsibility as near as possible to the client has been re-garded as an important aspect of care management.

All Scottish authorities have made plans for some degree of budgetary devolution. In the majority of cases, community care budgets, whether for residential or community-based services, are currently held by district or divisional managers. While some regions were cautious about devolving budgets further, Highland, Central and Orkney have plans to devolve budgets to team leaders. Only Western Isles is currently speaking of devolution to individual care managers. Throughout, however, there is a concern to increase the financial awareness of fieldwork staff, for example through training or working to shadow or notional budgets. Caution is often, however, a product of the developmental stage of financial account-ing and information systems and of the annuality of local authority budgets rather than an opposition to devolution *per se*. The Audit Com-mission (1992) warned that failure to address such parameters is tanta-mount to 'courting disaster'. Two regions spoke of a proportion of the budget having to be retained at the centre to support a few very costly packages.

Several regions give individual care managers an element of flexibility by devolving a small part of the budget to the team – 'giving permission to be imaginative at local level' as it was described in one region. Dumfries and Galloway, for example, have devolved fifteen per cent of their share of Department of Social Security transfer moneys to area teams. Half the sum is intended to help specific individuals with complex needs to remain in their own homes. The remainder can be used to commission new services. In Lothian each of the twenty practice teams has received £30,000 from infrastructure costs to provide domiciliary support.

Detailed implementation
The models outlined above are those articulated by respondents at the strategic planning level. As with any policy initiative, however, the reality has to be examined at the frontline. The main phase of the Social Work Research Centre evaluation of the new arrangements includes detailed examination of the implementation of assessment and care management in four authorities, two examples of both Model 1 and Model 2. Individual case monitoring will reveal the detailed processes involved in care management, together with both client and service outcomes, while interviews with the care managers or co-ordinators will explore both general principles of care management and, at a second interview, focus on the detail of practice in individual cases. The first round of these interviews is under way at the time of writing and therefore only the most preliminary of observations can be made.

Increasingly evident, however, is that whatever the clarity of the models presented above, at individual and team level there is considerable diversity of practice. Individuals may be working to their own remits; where policies are shared more widely, they are often under continual reinterpretation or revision. The uncertainties and discrepancies that abound first became evident when we approached teams to organise the fieldwork, bringing with us the relatively straightforward concepts of the models outlined above. In many instances ground practice appeared to bear little relationship to what might pass as the regional policy. Indeed in certain areas our exposition of what we thought to be agreed policy proved a catalyst for extensive discussion.

It is perhaps useful to headline a few of the issues emerging in interviews with care managers. Perhaps most fundamental is the uncertainty amongst individuals as to the exact nature of the new concept. Early exposition of national guidelines was often difficult to relate to local practice. Moreover, a time lag could be present between different operational levels within the one region. Responses devised at a strategic level may not have filtered down; alternatively, the understanding operative at the front-line may subsequently have been revised.

Transition from service led assessment to a system responsive to need demands a shift in mind-set whose magnitude should not be underestimated. In the words of one manager 'we talk a very good game'. Even at the stage of selecting service responses, individuals speak of being constrained in their choices because of uncertainty, perhaps as to the quality of an unfamiliar resource. It requires more than financial resources alone to provoke the innovative or merely non-standard response. Indeed, even with budgetary control, the care managers in the EPIC project found innovation difficult to achieve (Bland and Hudson 1994).

A number of care managers report that additional assessments at the stage of service provision continue, for example by occupational therapy or home care. Moreover, there appears to be considerable variation between both individuals and areas in the nature of care plans. Systematic examination of this variation will be required.

As the tasks of care management progress, individuals or teams may find themselves having to clarify areas of uncertainty. For example, there is considerable variation in the practice following initial assessment. One region, for example, closes cases once the care plan is in place; another practises a very different policy in that no case should be closed while services either provided or funded are continuing, or where there is a review pending. Various options are being explored, however, perhaps 'diaring' a case pending review, or distinguishing 'active' and 'passive' mode cases. Where there is more intense activity, one region has spoken of appointing a 'care coordinator' to carry out day-to-day monitoring.

Implementation of care management may also reveal considerable variation according to specific care group. In a specialist mental health team, for example, in a good proportion of the cases for which a complex assessment is begun it is discontinued, perhaps because of a change in mental state or a refusal of the care package. Models of care management may need to be varied according to such exigencies.

The picture beginning to emerge from the current monitoring is closely replicated by that reported in the JICC study identifying training needs for care management (1993). Indeed the conclusion from that exercise that 'there are as many different models of care management in practice as there are Social Services Departments', is closely echoed by one of the Scottish care managers who spoke of 'as many different definitions of care management as there are care workers'. Amongst its recommendations, this report suggests a need to identify nationally agreed and recognised competencies for care management, and highlights the need for senior management clarity and vision as to where the organisation is going if those undertaking care management activities are not to become confused.

The pattern outlined is perhaps no more than should be expected at this stage in the implementation of major change. There does, however, need to be further clarification of the degree to which the front-line responses in different regions accord with the strategic intent. Moreover, and it is to be hoped that the SWRC research will provide this, there needs to be elaboration of the extent to which the different models are equally effective in terms of delivering the core tasks of care management.

Acknowledgements

I would like to express my appreciation to colleagues at the Social Work Research Centre whose work on the project has contributed to the preparation of this chapter.

References

Audit Commission (1992) *Community Care: Managing the Cascade of Change.* London: HMSO.

Beardshaw, V. and Towell, D. (1990) *Assessment and Care Management: Implications for the Implementation of 'Caring for People'.* London: King's Fund Institute.

Bland, R. and Hudson, H. (1994) *EPIC: Providing Home Support to Frail Elderly People.* Stirling: Social Work Research Centre, University of Stirling.

Buglass, D. (1993) *Assessment and Care Management: A Scottish Overview of Impending Change. Community Care in Scotland Discussion Paper Number 2.* Stirling: Social Work Research Centre, University of Stirling.

Cambridge, P. (1992) 'Case management in community services: organizational responses.' *British Journal of Social Work 22,* 495–517.

Challis, D. and Davies, B. (1986) *Case Management in Community Care.* Aldershot: Gower.

Challis, D., Chessum, R., Chesterman, J., Luckett, R. and Woods, B. (1988) 'Community care for the frail elderly: an urban experiment.' *British Journal of Social Work 18,* (Supplement)43–54.

Challis, D., Darton, R., Johnston, L., Stone, M., Traske, K. and Wall, B. (1989) *Supporting Frail Elderly People at Home: The Darlington Community Care*

Project. Canterbury: Personal Social Services Research Unit, University of Kent at Canterbury.

Dant, T. and Gearing, B. (1990) 'Keyworkers for elderly people in the community: case managers and care co-ordinators.' *Journal of Social Policy* 19, 331–360.

Department of Health (1990) *Community Care in the Next Decade and Beyond: Policy Guidance*. London: HMSO.

Department of Health, Social Services Inspectorate and Scottish Office, Social Work Services Group (1991a) *Care Management and Assessment: Managers' Guide*. London: HMSO.

Department of Health, Social Services Inspectorate and Scottish Office, Social Work Services Group (1991b) *Care Management and Assessment: Practitioners Guide*. London: HMSO.

Grampian Regional Council (1993) *Care Management Procedures and Standards*. Aberdeen: Grampian Regional Council Social Work Department.

Huxley, P. (1993) 'Case management and care management in community care.' *British Journal of Social Work* 23, 365–381.

Joint Initiative for Community Care (1993) *Care Management: Identifying the Training Needs*. Milton Keynes: Joint Initiative for Community Care.

Meethan, K., Thompson, C. and Parker, G. (1993) *Making it Happen? Care Management in Practice*. York: Social Policy Research Unit, University of York.

North, C. and Ritchie, J. (1993) *Factors Influencing the Implementation of the Care Programme Approach*. London: HMSO.

Onyett, S. (1992) *Care Management in Mental Health*. London: Chapman and Hall.

Petch, A., Stalker, K., Taylor, C. and Taylor, J (1994) *Assessment and Care Management Pilot Projects in Scotland: An Overview. Community Care in Scotland Discussion Paper No 3*. Stirling: Social Work Research Centre, University of Stirling.

Pilling, D. (1992) *Approaches to Case Management for People with Disabilities*. London: Jessica Kingsley Publishers.

Richardson, A. and Higgins, R. (1990) *Care Management in Practice: Reflections on the Wakefield Care Management Project*. Leeds: Nuffield Institute for Health Service Studies, University of Leeds.

Schneider, J. (1993) 'Care programming in mental health: assimilation and adaptation'. *British Journal of Social Work* 23, 383–403.

Scottish Office (1994) *Community Care: A Role for Housing* (draft). Edinburgh: Scottish Office.

Smale, G. and Tuson, G. (1993) *Empowerment, Assessment, Care Management and the Skilled Worker*. London: Practice and Development Exchange, National Institute for Social Work.

Stalker, K., Taylor. J., and Petch. A. (1994) *Implementing Community Care in Scotland: Early Snapshots. Community Care in Scotland Discussion Paper No 4*. Stirling: Social Work Research Centre, University of Stirling.

Taylor, E, Scott, L. and Rowley, D. (1993) *Grampian Pilot Projects: Evaluation Report*. Dundee: Department of Social Work, University of Dundee.

Chapter 2

Assessing and Managing Care
What Future for the Independent Sector?

Stephen Maxwell and Mike Titterton

A principal challenge now facing voluntary and private sector agencies is the need to respond to developments in assessment and care management. This chapter reviews the current position based on a survey of 25 independent sector organisations and considers emerging models of practice.

Policy for the independent sector

The guidance

Government policy statements on community care have been consistent in leaving scope for the involvement of voluntary agencies in the 'needs' assessment of community care clients. The White Paper *Caring for People: community care in the next decade and beyond* (1989) envisaged the involvement of a range of agencies in assessment under the lead responsibility of the local authority. The official Scottish Office and Department of Health guidance on care management and assessment allows for the involvement of independent agencies in assessment. *Community Care in Scotland: Assessment and Care Management* (Scottish Office 1991a) states boldly: 'All relevant agencies should be involved in the assessment and subsequent decision taking process before commitments are made.' Or again:

> 'Voluntary organisations may be involved in the assessment process either by undertaking assessments in specialised fields on behalf of local authorities or through individual professional workers who have a particular contribution to make because they have specialist

knowledge or have an existing or prospective involvement in the provision of care.' (Scottish Office 1991a, p.10)

In the same permissive spirit *Care Management and Assessment: summary of practice guidance* (Department of Health/Scottish Office 1991b) states: 'In order to take account of all relevant needs, assessment may bring together contributions from a number of other specialists or agencies' (p.9).

By implication, the guidance extends the voluntary sector's role beyond assessment to embrace care management.

> 'Where the provision of a community care service is undertaken by a voluntary body on behalf of the local authority it must be clearly established whether their role extends into the field of assessment and if so what discretion they are entitled to use in reaching decisions to provide services to individual people on the local authority's behalf. It should be clear however in such arrangements that the ultimate responsibility for reaching decisions on service provision has to remain with the local authority.' (Scottish Office 1991b, p.12)

This implies that voluntary organisations might be involved not only in assessment but in care management with at least some devolved budgetary powers.

The role of the independent sector

The voluntary sector certainly had an expectation that the expanded role for the independent sector described in the Griffiths Report (1988) and the White Paper would extend across the range of community care functions from consultation in planning to the final delivery of services to the user. After all, in one authority or another voluntary organisations had been active across the range of community care functions prior to the NHS and Community Care Act. Indeed the sector's long championing of care in the community had bred a proprietorial attitude to the very concept. Voluntary organisations believed they were the main repositories of practical experience of care in the community. They had an unmatched knowledge of the different areas of specialist need and the practical experience of mobilising community resources, including volunteers, to meet those needs. It would be downright contradictory of the government to endorse the concept of community care only to impose a policy framework which limited the contribution which voluntary organisations could make from their wide and varied experience.

Yet one key principle of the government's policy did imply significant limitations in practice to the role of voluntary organisations in community care. That principle was the separation of powers, expressed most clearly in the purchaser-provider split.

The purchaser-provider split was designed to ensure first that major spending decisions were based on strategic priorities rather than on the sectional interests of professionals and providers and second that lines of accountability were clear. Applied to the health service, the principle has inspired the internal market of hospital and healthcare trusts, budget-holding hospital departments, GP fundholders and private sector providers. While the community care counterpart, the mixed economy of care, has been pushed less vigorously by the Government, particularly in Scotland, it is based on the same principles. As the local authority extends its purchasing role, it is expected progressively to surrender its provider role to the independent sector of for profit and non-profit agencies.

This principle of the separation of functions extends, however, to other community care roles. As a purchaser – and at least in the early years of care in the community a continuing provider of volume services – the local authority service department could not be relied on to be an impartial inspector of the quality of service. The separatist logic points to independent inspection. But economy, and the prospect of the erosion of the local authority's service role, led to a compromise in which local authorities were required to create an 'arms-length' inspection reporting directly to the social work director. If the purchasing and service functions were in conflict with the inspection role, then they might be in tension with other community care functions such as advocacy. And what about the placing of assessment and care management in the organisational spectrum of community care functions?

As the lead bodies for care in the community, local authorities have devised varying responses to these issues (see Alison Petch's chapter in this volume). For practical reasons if for none other, the local authorities continue to perform the whole range of community care functions, including service delivery. But their dealings with voluntary organisations are increasingly informed by an awareness of the principle and the putative advantages of separating community care functions.

Except in the case of residential homes for elderly people and nursing homes, the private (for profit) sector plays a minor role in community care provision in Scotland. In 1990, 20 per cent of residents of residential homes were accommodated in the private sector compared to 25 per cent in the voluntary sector and 55 per cent in the local authority sector; 47.5 per cent of residents in nursing homes were in private homes. The private sector also supplied a small number of places for people suffering mental illness and people with learning disabilities (Scottish Office 1991a). The main growth areas for private provision appear to be domiciliary nursing and care. The expected publication early in 1995 of the third edition of a Scottish Office Statistical Bulletin on Community Care will reveal the extent to which private sector community care provision has grown in recent years.

The impact of contracts

The replacement by local authorities of their grant funding of voluntary organisations by more highly specified contracts might have provided the opportunity for a formalisation of voluntary organisations' role in community care. In the two or three years immediately preceding the implementation of the NHS and Community Care Act, the voluntary sector persuaded itself that the contract culture was about to hit it with the impact of a 'Big Bang'(Maxwell 1989). In the event, while more highly specified contracts became the norm in some areas of voluntary sector involvement such as vocational training, in community care the advance of contracting has been very much slower. By the summer of 1994 community care contracts were still more conspicuous by their absence than their presence. The director of one major Scottish voluntary organisation providing £3 million worth of services for people with severe learning disabilities declared that he had yet to see a contract. And another organisation which had invested considerable resources in equipping itself for the advent of contracts, including a study trip to the United States, had to discontinue the post of contracts officer it had filled one year earlier because of a lack of contracts.

The one source that was expected to generate an increased flow of contracts in the near future was the hospital discharge programme. Even here, however, there were concerns about the nature of the contracts. While 'spot' or 'mini' contracts for individual service users were favoured by some health boards and social work purchasers, voluntary organisations favoured block contracts. Block contracts alone provided organisations with a degree of flexibility and a base for development, albeit a narrow one. Without block contracts many organisations feared that the multifunctional role endorsed by Griffiths and the White Paper would rapidly wither and die.

The slow advance of contracting has meant that voluntary organisations have lacked a key opportunity to engage local authorities in formal discussion of the roles they might play in community care. Instead organisations reported that the social work authorities were too preoccupied with the immediate demands of establishing community care processes and systems, and with overcoming early operational problems, to give serious consideration to the potential roles of voluntary organisations. Some voluntary organisations, including the Church of Scotland's Board of Social Responsibility – the largest independent provider of residential care – faced with a financial 'care gap' of £4 million a year, shared this local authority preoccupation with operational issues. Other organisations were, as clearly, frustrated by it. It seems plausible to conclude that in the absence of a formal consideration of the role voluntary organisations might play, local authorities in this first year of community care implementation tended to impose on their voluntary sector partners a largely undigested understanding of the Government's view of community care functions.

A survey of Scottish voluntary organisations

A survey of voluntary sector and private sector organisations in Scotland was undertaken as research for this chapter. In the absence of any directory or register of independent community care providers, no systematic sample was possible. Instead, a selection of twenty-five agencies was made, embracing providers of widely differing scale, operating at national, regional and local levels in Scotland and including providers of residential care and domiciliary services for elderly infirm people, people with severe learning disabilities, people with physical disabilities, people with visual and aural disabilities, and HIV/AIDS sufferers. Interviews were held usually with a single senior officer with responsibility for negotiating agreements with purchasers. The evidence from these sources is consistent with the evidence available from the authors' continuing contacts with a wide range of voluntary sector community care providers.

Telephone interviews, supplemented by some face-to-face interviews, were held with key respondents in each agency, either the director or the development officer. The survey was undertaken in the period June –

August 1994. Respondents were asked about the present position in respect of assessment and care management developments and to identify and discuss pressing issues. Respondents were also asked about the state of contracts.

Only one contact with the private care sector was made, albeit the representative of the private care home owners in Scotland. The response was clear that the private sector's involvement in assessment and care management was insignificant.

Assessment

Of the agencies surveyed, many pointed out that the process was really only getting under way – despite it being some 14 months after the implementation date of April 1993. A number of respondents complained of lengthy delays and slow progress in getting people assessed and referred on to them under the new system.

One consequence of the local authorities' approach appears to have been a tendency to define voluntary organisations as service providers. One organisation in west central Scotland (Voluntary Association for Mental Welfare, Motherwell) reported that since the introduction of community care it had lost its access to multi-agency networking and information through the disbandment of a resources allocation group convened by the social work department to discuss individual cases. The department had explained that under the new community care regime 'providers should not be on a group like the resources allocation group.'

A major voluntary agency in the north of Scotland reported that the social work department wished to terminate a twelve month pilot arrangement under which the agency used its own social work staff to carry out assessments for residential care homes in the area while accepting social work assessments for its own homes. As part of a reorganisation of its adult care, the social work department wished to create a single route assessment through its own adult care teams.

An agency in the east of Scotland providing services for people with severe learning difficulties reported that where previously it had carried out its own assessments, the process was now firmly owned by the social work department. Another reported the instance of a local authority social worker insisting that he was required to chair a multi-agency, multi-disciplinary assessment team 'by law'. Yet another reported a tendency for social work department care managers to invoke their status as purchasing authorities in disputes over assessment of needs – 'Come on now, we're the ones who are paying.'

There were a few exceptions to this marginalising of voluntary organisations in community care assessment. These were found mainly in long established agencies serving traditional client groups such as blind or visually impaired people or people with hearing disabilities. One such agency reported contracts with two social work authorities to provide the range of community care services including assessment, service provision and management for users of its highly specialised service. Another reported a service agreement to carry out full assessments and provide care management, though this excluded budget holding. In both the arrangements were under review. Also, service specific assessments are being carried out by some agencies with a limited function: Crossroads Care Attendant Scheme is one example.

Another long-established agency, the Scottish Council for Spastics, undertook specialist assessment services for social work departments by agreement. But it is clear from responses from other organisations that the possession of specialist expertise by itself did not guarantee a significant role in assessment. They complained that while insisting on their statutory role local authority social workers often lacked the specialist expertise. Several of the organisations declared a determination to press for an enhanced role in assessment whenever they could persuade the local authority to extend its concern from maintaining the system to developing it to maximise the contribution of all its actors.

If voluntary organisations played a modest, and usually diminishing, role in the initial assessments at the point at which the client entered the community care system, they maintained a significant stake in other stages of assessment. The majority carried out their own assessments parallel to the formal social work assessment. Examples include Alzheimer's Scotland – Action on Dementia which, through its local projects, provide services for people with dementia and their carers; Margaret Blackwood Housing Association, a provider of specially designed houses for physically disabled people; and Richmond Fellowship Scotland which promotes the integration into the community of people with a mental illness. In some cases, local authority social workers filled in the voluntary organisation's assessment forms at the same time as they filled in the authority's form. In cases where an organisation like Crossroads Care Attendant Scheme provided services in a user's house this was a legal requirement for the indemnification of their own workers. Whatever the nature of their funding agreement, all the organisations retained a right of veto on the acceptance of an assessed client, though recognising the possible financial impact in the short term where they operated 'spot' contracts or the longer-term consequences where they had block contracts. And a number, mainly those whose services were less costly, insisted on their determination to take clients who had not gone through the social work assessments. Another area where voluntary organisations retained a role was in review assessments carried out in collaboration with social work departments and other agencies. The only formal involvement private, for-profit organisations appeared to have was in follow-up assessment, after the client's admission to residential care.

Provision for homeless people deserves to be treated as a special case. At the start of the community care regime, the assessment process in place was quickly revealed as completely inappropriate for homeless people. Under pressure from voluntary organisations, regional councils in Scotland introduced a system under which providers of emergency accommodation were able to secure a 'fast-track' assessment (usually within seven days) for their emergency admissions. While the provider was given no guarantee that the social work authority would cover the costs incurred prior to the assessment for clients who were subsequently assessed as not being in need, the system has worked well. The record suggests that where a problem registers high on the 'crisis' scale, in this case with an imminent danger of voluntary agencies collapsing and vulnerable youngsters being decanted on to the street, the local authorities' community care systems have the capacity to respond effectively.

Emerging models in assessment

The range of practice in assessment can be summarised:

(1) *exclusive* – where assessment is exclusively a function of the social work department.

(2) *combined* – where the social worker uses a form agreed with the voluntary organisation or fills in a voluntary organisation form as well as a social work department form.

(3) *parallel* – where the social work department's assessment is paralleled by a separate voluntary organisation assessment.

(4) *secondment* – where a local authority social worker is seconded to a voluntary organisation to carry out assessments, adopting a combined approach in most cases.

(5) *devolved* – where the voluntary organisation has powers under a contract or service agreement to act as the agent for the social work department.

(6) *independent* – where a voluntary organisation carries out its own assessment as part of its own referral process with no expectation of public funding for the client.

Current practice was heavily weighted towards the 'exclusive' end of the spectrum.

Overall, the survey found that assessment was clearly perceived as the 'trigger to resources' or the key to the community care system. Assessments were slow and bureaucratic, involving increased paperwork and administration. The voluntary sector was stereotyped as a service provider and its expertise in assessment discounted.

Care management

The main findings point even more strongly to the exclusion of independent sector agencies from care management. Care management is, as the guidance indicates, intended to be clearly linked to the assessment process. It was therefore anticipated that the role of voluntary and private sector organisations would be relatively minor but that there might be scope for different kinds of involvement in care management arrangements.

The voluntary sector's role in the wider field of care management reflects the limitations of its role in assessment. Typically, voluntary organisations are excluded from care management. Whether or not the assessment process involved a parallel assessment or any significant input from the voluntary organisation, clients are referred to voluntary organisations with a package of care determined by the purchasing authority and under the authority's management control. One organisation reported that it had gone to considerable pains two years ago to draw up a menu of services with carefully itemised costs, including management costs: it was still pressing for information about its menu to be included in the region's community care database.

With so little involvement in care management it is not surprising that there was no voluntary sector involvement in the management of care budgets. Even where an organisation had a formal service agreement with the regional council to provide a care assessment and management package for its own specialised services it had no control over the budget. One such organisation reported that differences at the district level between social work managers created difficulties for their own budgeting.

In sum, the evidence from our survey suggests that very few exceptions to exclusion from care management existed. However, there evidently was scope for independent sector care management on specialist projects, for example Edinvar's Brain Injuries Project. Many agencies claimed that they had a parallel or similar care management system – sometimes in embryonic form – operating within their own set-ups.

A small number of agencies stated that they would 'not be unhappy' with a care management role delegated by the social work department. However, some respondents were evidently worried about crossing or blurring the lines between the role of the care manager as a kind of advocate and the role of the provider. Some felt that they might be placed in an awkward or compromising position if agency staff took on a care management role, in addition to their responsibilities for providing care.

Our survey supports the judgement of Stirling University observers (Stalker, Taylor and Petch 1994) that:

> 'The new arrangements for care management appear to have had little impact on the voluntary sector so far: their "service providing" identity is seen as limiting the extent to which they can act as care managers or carry out holistic "needs led" assessments.' (p.29)

Adapting to the new environment

A number of organisations are giving serious thought to adapting the principle of the separation of powers as a way of extending the range of their involvement in community care. Perhaps the most notable initiative in 1993 was the creation of the Independent Needs Assessment and Advocacy Service (Scotland) (INAASS), a limited company with charitable status and with funding from the Housing Associations' Charitable Trust, the Borders Regional Council and the Penumbra Development Trust. INAASS's remit is to offer individuals with mental health problems who are having difficulty in obtaining appropriate help from social work departments, a range of services embracing information on services and users' networks; assessment by an experienced social worker; representation by a social worker or by another service user in having their Needs Assessment and Care Management plans reviewed and revised; help with complaints procedures and the protection of civil and legal rights; and the development of self-advocacy. The Service focused initially on the Borders and Lothian Regions but its objective is to create a national service. It bases its claim for support on its unique status as an independent source of professional scrutiny and advocacy focused on Needs Assessments. From this independent base INAASS hopes to play a key role in providing checks and balances and in influencing care management. Another major service providing agency is also considering setting up an arms-length specialised advocacy service. The director of a leading housing association also commented that the way ahead for the voluntary sector lay in sponsoring an independent voluntary sector as-sessment agency. Yet another service providing agency has revealed ambitions to develop a monitoring and inspection role under contract to its local authority.

The application of the logic of the purchaser-provider split to the wider range of community care functions is forcing voluntary organisations to confront issues created by their growth as service providers. Many of the organisations which are now major providers began life as policy lobby-ists, representative groups or general support groups. They retained a wide range of these functions as they developed their service providing capacity. The growth of service agreements and the prospect of contracts poses a direct challenge to this multi-function role, as the Griffiths report itself anticipated. One danger is that service contracts might explicitly restrict other activities; another is self-censorship by organisations fearful of antagonising major funders; another is the creation of an imbalance in the ethos and management of organisations as market-led management specialists came to dominate professional staff. If these dangers imply a separation of functions into different organisations, as the CENTRIS report *Voluntary Action* (Knight 1993) proposed, many in the voluntary sector insist on the merits of maintaining a common organisational base for the different functions. A common base would ensure that the practical knowledge of the service providers would be quickly fed through to the policy lobbyists; that the insights of the counsellors or advocates would be immediately accessible to the development staff; that new policy thinking would continually challenge the routines of service providers; and not least that the lobbyists and campaigners would have the stability and financial strength of the service providing function behind them.

This belief in the merits of integration is clearly reflected in the com-plaints voiced by voluntary organisations that assessments are often made by social work department staff less knowledgeable and experienced in the special needs areas than their own workers, sometimes with reference to criteria which are simply irrelevant to the services offered by the voluntary organisation. It is interesting, too, that the most notable reorganisation among voluntary sector community care agencies in Scotland in 1993 was the merger of the campaigning body Scottish Action on Dementia (SAD) with Alzheimer's Scotland, whose lead function was service provision. Among the reasons were to secure a wider base for campaigning and to promote the authority of the merged Alzheimer's Scotland-Action on Dementia as a contributor to public policy debate.

Conclusion

The growth of the mixed economy of care and the threat of contracting seem then to create a tension for voluntary organisations. Purchasers in the shape of central and local government demand the organisational separation of functions, which conflicts with a strong impulse on the part of voluntary organisations to maintain the traditional linkage between their diverse functions even as they compete to extend their role in the emerging new care market.

The capacity of voluntary organisations to reconcile these two aims will be determined initially by the purchasing authorities. There is no reason in the community care legislation why social work authorities should deny voluntary organisations a wider range of roles in community care. In principle, a decentralised mixed economy of care can provide assessment, care management, or advocacy as easily as it provides direct care services. Of course local authorities may have political reasons to maintain a virtual monopoly of certain functions. Along with inspection, assessment and care management are the control functions of the community care system. To decentralise these functions by contracting them out means creating centres of knowledge and expertise outwith the direct management control of the purchasers. Even where the purchasers imposed an organisational separation between direct care providers and providers of assessment, care management or advocacy, the new independent providers would be members of the wider constituencies of private for-profit providers or far more likely, of voluntary sector providers. They would contribute their knowledge to the sector's internal debates and share the sector's inheritance of values.

Local authorities might still from political belief choose to decentralise their community care functions, contenting themselves with the roles of the planning and purchasing authority and developing a role as last resort champions of the interests of the user against the expanding ranks of the independent sector service providers. They will certainly be under continued pressure from the government's policy in competitive tendering as well as its community care policy to promote a mixed economy of care. In Scotland the drastic reduction in the size of most social work authorities as a result of the imminent reorganisation of local government may very well reinforce the pressure.

In this perspective, many voluntary organisations see the prospect of contracting as an opportunity rather than a threat. They believe it will carry purchasers, in particular local authorities, beyond the current stage of limiting voluntary organisations to a service provider role and stimulate them into thinking more creatively about the range of roles which voluntary organisations might fill in community care. Most voluntary organisations have retained an ambition to have a role in assessment and in care management, as well as in planning, advocacy and inspection. They point to the inconsistency of local authorities imposing a separation of functions on others while themselves continuing to be multifunctional as purchasers, providers, inspectors, assessors, care managers, advocates and, of course, frequent commentators on policy. They see the new guidance on community care plans (Scottish Office 1994) with its call for a shift of emphasis from the processes of community care planning to costed purchasing plans, as helping to move local authorities from the first, somewhat introspective phase of community care provision into a second phase which is at once more practical and more inventive. And they seem willing themselves to meet the organisational challenges of the new market by experimenting with new structures and relationships within the sector.

References

Caring for People: Community Care In the Next Decade and Beyond (1989). Cm 849. London: HMSO.

Department of Health, Social Services Inspectorate and Scottish Office, Social Work Services Group (1991) *Care Management and Assessment: Practitioners' Guide*. London: HMSO.

Griffiths, R. (1988) *Community Care: Agenda for Action*. London: HMSO.

Knight, B. (1993) *Voluntary Action*. London: CENTRIS and Home Office.

Maxwell, S. (1989) *Riding the Tiger: The Scottish voluntary sector in the market economy*. Edinburgh: Scottish Council for Voluntary Organisations.

Scottish Office (1991a) Community Care In Scotland: Assessment and Care
    Management. Circular, SW11/1991 HHD/DGM (1991) 40.
Scottish Office (1991b) *Statistical Bulletin: Community Care Bulletin*. Edinburgh:
    Scottish Office, Social Work Services Group.
Scottish Office (1994) Community Care Plans, Community Care
    Implementation Unit draft circular No SW.
Stalker K., Taylor J. and Petch, A. (1994) Implementing Community Care In
    Scotland: Early Snapshots. Community Care in Scotland Discussion Paper
    No.4. Stirling: Social Work Research Centre, University of Stirling.

Chapter 3

Care Management Practice
Lessons from the USA

Phyllis J. Sturges

Introduction

As local authorities throughout the UK continue the implementation of
care management it is well to look at the research experience of the USA
in what is there called 'case management'. Since the mid 1970s case
management has produced many findings and also generated controversy. Much has been learned through trial and error. The UK has as much
to learn from the mistakes as from the successes of 20 years of experiments
in the USA. This chapter will summarise some of the research about major
elements of practice. It will not focus on the management of case management systems: a distinction which is all too often confused.

In the USA the research picture is complex and sometimes contradictory for several reasons. First, case management has been ill defined and
sporadically implemented. As Davies (1992) has said, 'the history of case
management has not been a continuous and coherent implementation of
a clear national policy' (p.120). This fact has created difficult problems for
researchers who attempt to do meta-research by comparing results from
different programs. Unlike the UK, there has been no White Paper or
Community Care Act as statements of national policy from which systems
could be developed for a whole range of vulnerable adults. Instead, pilot
projects began in scattered locations in the 1970s, large systems were
developed in the 1980s, and now case management is being widely used
with a whole range of populations. A great deal of evaluation research has
been done but studies have varied considerably in their size, sophistica-
tion and rigor (Rothman 1992).

A second factor is that case management developed not as a widely based response to vulnerable adults as in the UK, but rather in separate systems which have tended to have little contact with each other. This reflects the way that social and health services are organised in the USA. There is, for example, a large literature on work in long term care, and another on work with the severely mentally ill. However, until recently researchers in the two systems have not cited one another's work, have used different models and different instruments. These differences will be described in more detail further on.

While there is a good deal of research on older people and those with mental illness, there is much less on case management practice with other groups of adults, specifically those with learning difficulties, the younger physically disabled, AIDS patients and substance abusers. However, reports of studies are scattered among so many journals that this generalisation must be qualified. For the purposes of this discussion, however, the literature on practice with older people and the mentally ill will be highlighted because it is the most comprehensive.

Third, there has been insufficient research among all groups about case management practice processes and the impact of organisational contexts on the work of case managers. This is particularly true of long term care. As a result, we have a great deal of information about client outcomes but much less about what case managers do or do not do with clients that contributes to these outcomes and how organisational environments impact worker effectiveness. It is striking to compare the US literature about case management with older people with the influential work of Challis and Davies (1986) writing about the model projects developed by the Personal Social Services Research Unit (PSSRU). In the latter there is much more attention to practice processes. However, much of the writing in the UK since the implementation of the new policy has not been so discerning. The PSSRU's 'clinical' and 'complete' approach to long term care management seems to have given way to an 'administrative model' being practised in local authorities (Challis, Chesterman, Traske and von Abendorff 1990, Huxley 1993). Perhaps this development was inevitable when care management was implemented nationally, but the implications are disturbing.

In summary, the literature on case management in the USA has been a confusing one, and insufficient attention has been given to comparison of findings between groups, to practice processes, and to organisational contexts. This is understandable given a history of unclear policy directives, the way social and health services are organised, and the subject itself, which has only become better understood over time. What is truly remarkable, however, is how case management systems and practice have grown and flourished in the midst of it all (Austin 1992, Rothman 1992).

History
Case management in the US evolved out of social work, public health, and community psychiatry. It developed in the 1970s for most of the same reasons that it has in the UK: in order better to co-ordinate community based services, to deter premature institutionalisation and/or unnecessary hospitalisation, to improve the quality of people's lives, and above all, to contain costs.

Some have argued that it was also developed as a substitute for adequate resources and structural reforms in community-based services. Rothman (1992) has suggested that the introduction of case managers with the severely mentally ill in the 1970s deflected attention from the issue of insufficient resources. Austin (1990) has argued that case management programs in long-term care have been popular because they use case managers to attack system problems while leaving the systems basically unchanged.

Because case management has been expected to be cost effective, workers in the US have frequently been caught between trying to meet the genuine needs of clients with inadequate resources and cost constraints. This analysis is relevant for the UK given the current crisis in adequate resourcing for community care. Care managers are expected to do needs led assessments and offer user choice while case loads are growing, users are being charged at higher rates, and services are increasingly rationed. Such a scenario leads inevitably, as it has in the US, to the scapegoating of case management and the social services in general for failing to deliver what was envisioned.

Because of the way social and health services have been organised in the US, community based services and benefits have been fragmented and difficult to access. Services and benefits are provided by a wide range of public and voluntary bodies, alongside private provision. Therefore, a major impetus for providing case management has been to assist clients and their families through the maze. Rose (1992) has said 'the need for case management constitutes an indictment of existing organisational and inter-organisational patterns of service design and delivery' (p.vii). Given high levels of fragmentation, case managers in the USA have been required to be advocates in order to insure that services were received by clients. Unlike the UK, they were less likely to have devolved budgets and to be purchasers of services. Instead, they have tended to operate more as brokers, meaning that they referred clients to services in the community and then tried to make sure that they received them (Applebaum and Austin 1990). Over time, however, the limitations of this approach have become evident and there has been movement towards more consolidated services and towards more purchasing by case managers. The On Lok model (Zawadski and Eng 1988) and its replications (Kane, Illston and Millar 1992) are examples of systems that give case managers more control over services since most are provided by the organisation. This trend is exactly the opposite of what is now occurring in the UK. The mixed economy of care and the purchaser provider split work against, not towards consolidation of services.

One does not see the same emphasis on advocacy in care management in the UK as in the USA. Perhaps this difference can be explained in part by the fact that the human services in the USA have traditionally resembled the mixed economy of care which the Conservative government has been so keen to develop. This analysis suggests that if, in the future, fewer services are provided by local authorities and more are contracted out, it will be increasingly difficult for consumers to understand where these services are and how to access them. The government has not recognised the degree to which a mixed economy of care can create access problems for users and carers. Multiple assessments, a chronic problem in the USA, and one that is beginning in the UK, are also more likely to occur in a mixed economy. If the USA experience is any guide, and present policy in the UK continues, there will be even more need for care managers in the future to bring more order to an increasingly fragmented system. Then care management becomes a symptom rather than a solution. The USA has responded to this dilemma by experimenting with more consolidation. Will the UK turn to it over time?

As a mixed economy of care develops, care managers will be required to be more assertive advocates, a role which in the past was left to the voluntary sector. Having the power to purchase a service does not guarantee that it will be provided well. How local authorities will both understand and support the need for advocacy by care managers remains to be seen. Findings from the DHSS demonstrations of the 1980s suggested that 'public sector case managers with advocacy responsibilities will find themselves accountable to both clients and the employing agency, risking conflicts and tensions' (Cambridge 1992, p.516).

Case management in the US has not been without its detractors. In long-term care, some have questioned its value based on extensive evaluation research which has not conclusively demonstrated its effectiveness (Callahan 1989). Others have suggested that the money used to provide this service in the mental health field might be better spent on other kinds of interventions or on increasing community resources available for clients (Franklin 1988). Still others have advocated giving money to clients to purchase what they need, in effect empowering them to be their own case managers.

Practice processes

There is a group of generic core tasks which case managers perform both in the USA and the UK. They are case finding, screening, assessment, care planning, co-ordination/linking, monitoring and reassessment/review. These core tasks are not as linear as supposed and frequently overlap (Rothman 1991). Evaluation is sometimes included as a core task for care managers in the USA but not in the UK. Needs led assessment has been more highly stressed in the UK. In the USA it is more taken for granted that professional practice is by definition needs led. That is an assumption, however, which has not been adequately tested (Kane 1992).

In the USA monitoring is viewed as crucial because it is essential to continuity of care and to prevention, major goals in long term work with vulnerable adults whose chronic conditions usually persist over time. The necessity for long-term work, and the practices required to do it successfully seem much less understood in the UK (Huxley 1991, Fisher 1991). In the past, much of the work with vulnerable adults has been crisis-oriented and short term: this is one of the reasons why care management was introduced. However, there is little evidence to suggest that there has yet been a shift in practice. Care managers in Scotland seemed confused about how to proceed after they finished the care coordination task and the way systems there are being organised only added to this confusion (Sturges 1994).

The Department of Health practice guidance (Department of Health 1991a, b) seems to have been responsible in part for the fact that practice got off to a confusing start. Effective monitoring requires a long term relationship between client and worker or team, beginning with the case finding, screening and assessment tasks, and continuing through until closure. The Guidance set up divisions which do not promote long term work. This issue is discussed further below.

Research in the USA has shown that practice skills needed by case managers are both direct and community based (Rothman 1991). Direct skills include a solid knowledge base about the group one is working with, the ability to engage and maintain a client and family's trust over time, to provide counselling as needed, to have a thorough knowledge of community resources, an ability to work well with other organisations, and the ability to advocate for and empower clients.

Less developed in the USA have been the community practice skills needed to develop needed resources proactively in local communities. True needs led care planning addresses not only what does exist, but also what does not. Community practice skills range from engaging and supervising volunteers and other community helpers, to developing coalitions to provide gap filling services (Sturges 1985). The interweaving of informal, quasi-formal and formal support is crucial to effective case management and is not reflected in the administrative model. Feiner (1994) has said the following about sources of care for the severely mentally ill: 'The most important question... is "who can I get to help?" Integral to our efforts should be the building of networks,... so that we can bolster the inevitably impoverished support systems of our patients' (p.22).

Developing local community resources takes time, but can result in cost savings (Sturges 1985, 1986). Certainly the cost effectiveness of the Kent project may have been due in part to the roles played by 'natural helpers'. The UK could profitably revisit its tradition of community social work for the contributions it could make to skill development in this area of practice. Additional staff who serve as resource developers for different teams is an experiment which should be tried. Most local authority care managers have little experience of this kind of work. They will need training from the voluntary sector which is much more experienced in community and advocacy skills.

A major difference in practice between the two countries has been the tendency in the UK to fragment the process. An example is the tendency to separate assessment from care management in the UK, a development which has not occurred in the USA. It is significant to note that this kind of splitting did not occur in the early model projects. However, care management as defined and described by government guidance has been characterised more by separating functions than by continuity, and shows the influence of changes in the health service. Assessment and care management are the terms used in the UK, but never in the USA, where case management is rightly seen as encompassing assessment.

The justification for splitting the two has been to insure that assessors are objective and do needs led assessments, since those implementing and monitoring care plans will be working within resource constraints. Huxley (1993) has been critical of this separation, suggesting that it demonstrates a lack of confidence in the professional judgement of the care manager. His observation has considerable merit and deserves more attention, because separating assessment and care management violates continuity and generally confuses understanding of this mode of practice. Moreover, there is no empirical evidence to support the separation and there is research evidence in both countries to show that a continuous and trusting relationship over time between worker or team and client leads to better outcomes (Eggert, Friedman and Zimmer 1990, Rapp and Chamberlin 1986, Challis and Davies 1986). Users and carers do not want to deal with different people. Care managers gain little professional satisfaction from only assessing and not being able to follow through. They cannot learn from their practice when they cannot see the long term results of their care plans (Huxley 1993). Separating functions also leads to unnecessary multiple assessments which are expensive, and frustrating for clients. There is some evidence that the most qualified care managers are being given assessor roles while those less qualified are then assigned the so called care manager role (Sturges 1994). This development is alarming and only contributes to lack of continuity of care and a continuation of poor practice from the past.

Another example of the tendency to fragment processes is the potential impact of the purchaser-provider split. A concept which was developed by accountants for the health service has now been applied to the social services. The purpose of the split, along with the instructions about contracting out and competitive tendering, appears to have much more to do with insuring that local authorities divest themselves of their services than with anything else. Its impact on practice cannot yet be fully understood, but it appears from this author's research to be causing considerable confusion both for managers and practitioners (Sturges 1994). The split has been interpreted in different ways by different local authorities and can work against continuity of care. It has already reduced the availability of skilled social work professionals for work with mentally retarded ill people (Huxley 1994).

Under the purchaser-provider split care managers are seen as purchasers, not as providers. That is generally true in all case management, since it is the co-ordinating rather than the provider role that is paramount. However, it is also true that depending on the model used, care managers may also need to be providers of some services. Case managers in the USA in mental health are providing clinical management, skills training, and developing resources for clients (Witheridge 1992). In work with older people it is well known that many clients resist being referred for counselling to outside agencies. Much of the supportive counselling needed by them and their carers is best provided by a skilled professional case manager. There has been resistance to letting case managers provide counselling in long term care in the USA and this has been one of the weaknesses of practice there (Sturges 1992).

For the UK to say that a care manager cannot be a provider confuses the process, and keeps practice from having the flexibility which it needs to have. The purchaser-provider split is an artificial macro construct which has nothing to do with micro practice in the human services and which is being imposed on a natural helping process.

Practice characteristics

Case management in the USA has grown a great deal in the past fifteen years and is now used in a wide range of settings and with many client groups including children and families. It can be found in community-based programs where most of the work is done in people's homes, in rehabilitation and day centres, and in hospitals and nursing homes. More recently it has been done as a type of private practice, predominantly by social workers and nurses in work with older people (Secord 1987).

Social workers and, increasingly, nurses are most likely to be case managers in long term care. In mental health work, social workers, psychiatric nurses, psychologists, and case assistants undertake it. Occupational therapists and home care organisers would be unlikely to do case management because of the nature of their training, and because they are usually not employed by social service agencies, community mental health centres or in discharge activities in hospitals. Para-professionals are sometimes used as case managers in the USA, in many cases in order to reduce costs. There is controversy about this practice.

It is generally agreed now in the USA that there is no one profession that can necessarily do case management best. The skills required have been identified, but all of the helping professions encompass them. What is required is competence in practising these skills. Competition between and among disciplines over which is best qualified to do case management is a futile activity. There is, however, an on-going debate about the level of education required and whether this is a method of practice which requires a high skill level. Some argue that educational levels should be high and that those with advanced education are able to function with less supervision (Kurtz, Bagarozzi and Pollane 1984). Lamb (1990) and Kanter (1985) have been persuasive advocates for the position that those who work with the severely mentally ill need to be able to provide psychotherapy as well as co-ordinating concrete services. In two studies by the author (Sturges 1985, 1986) case managers without graduate level training had difficulty working effectively with older people who had mental health and substance abuse problems. Others, however, argue that paraprofessionals perform better because unlike professionals they are more likely to get out of their offices, focus on the concrete needs of clients and advocate for them (Rose 1992). Para-professionals are frequently used as case managers in work with underserved minority groups. Bilingual, bicultural case managers are crucial to reaching certain groups and there are not enough of them as yet with professional qualifications. Volunteers can work successfully with certain tasks of case management such as screening, information giving, referring for routine services and monitoring. However, they require good supervision and training from professionals (Sturges 1985, 1986).

The debate over skill levels is part of the larger issue about what roles case managers should assume in their work. Some have defined this practice as primarily brokering concrete services for clients and little more: the so-called administrative model. From this perspective paraprofessionals could do it as well as anyone else. However, the administrative model has little appeal for qualified social workers since their well honed assessment and counselling skills cannot be used. This creates a morale problem and in some cases a flight into other types of work. Case management has lower status in the USA than many other modes of social work and educators often don't teach it very well, but this situation is improving. The National Association of Social Workers (1992) has defined case management as a distinct mode of practice, and has issued practice standards which require a high level of expertise.

The nature of client need should determine the skill level required. Practice with more complex client situations requires higher levels of professional expertise, including a substantive knowledge base about the group being served (Steinberg and Carter 1983). However, there is considerable variability around the country in the skill levels of case managers, even when they are working with the same kinds of groups and client problems. In mental health case managers do more clinically focused work but there is no reason to suppose that frail older people do not also require a high level of expertise because of the complex interactions between their physical and emotional states. Ageist attitudes have interfered with raising the standard of clinical work done in case management in long-term care. Older people are often considered unacceptable candidates for therapy: this is a long standing and intractable problem in the USA.

The debate over who should be doing care management and the skill levels required is also occurring in the UK. The PSSRU models used qualified social workers with experience in work with older people in Kent, and qualified professionals from other disciplines as well in Gateshead and Darlington. Both their client and cost outcomes were consistently positive. However, since the implementation of care management nation-wide, local authorities are using a greater variety of disciplines and skill levels. It is important for more substantive evaluation research to be done in this area. The relationships between the independent variables of skill level, knowledge base and experience on the dependent variables of client outcomes and cost effectiveness are not well understood in either country.

The organisational context in which care managers practice has also been considerably neglected by research. The support and status, including pay, which organisations give to case managers are important. So is the quality of the supervision available.

A major development in the human services in the USA has been the introduction of extensive information systems to insure accountability. This development has resulted in unacceptably high levels of paper work for many case managers who do extensive assessments and order numerous services. Case managers believe that filling out forms takes away from the time they could more profitably be spending with clients and research has borne this out (Caragonne 1981, Eggert, Zimmer, Hall and Friedman 1990). Unless information systems are well designed they obstruct rather than support practice, and have a negative effect on morale. As a result, many of the most competent people leave for other kinds of work. There is some evidence that this happening in the UK as well (Hugman 1994). Certainly it is important to know what things cost and to keep track of what is spent, but ways should be found for doing that without sacrificing the time required for monitoring and reassessing client need. User-friendly programs and clerical support for teams are needed, not tying care managers up interminably with desk work.

Case load size is still another important practice issue in both countries. Caseload size varies depending on the type of client and the complexity of need, but research in the USA has suggested that case loads in mental health that exceed forty are often associated with reactive rather than proactive work and with burnout (Intagliata 1992). There is, however, little research about caseload size in either country and this is an area requiring further work. Case loads are growing in the UK and there is debate over how many cases a care manager can reasonably be expected to cope with and much confusion about when cases should be closed. Fortunately, the Department of Health has invested in research on caseload size in both London and Manchester, and results could be important for practice (Huxley 1994).

Local authorities would be well advised to concentrate on outcomes rather than to be driven by numbers. Otherwise most people will be provided with a very poor service. Evaluation research will document this. Moreover, professional burnout is dysfunctional for everyone concerned, and constantly recruiting and retraining new case managers is expensive.

Limiting caseloads is easier said than done, however, given the political context of statutory work and the severe resource constraints. On the other hand, it is unreasonable for the health service to expect care managers to be able to respond quickly to referrals when they have too many cases. Yet that is what they and the general public seem to expect. Case management practice in the USA has suffered in those systems that seek the cheapest ways to deliver it, including poorly trained staff and excessive case loads. It would be unfortunate to see quality practice with vulnerable adults so compromised in the UK, but current trends are not too encouraging (Henwood 1994).

Financial means testing by care managers is another function which can be problematic. In the USA eligibility workers handle this as part of the screening process. In the UK this is not happening and care managers are expected to fill out complex financial forms as part of the assessment process. As a result they are falling behind in carrying out assessments and there is growing confusion between the screening and the assessment tasks (Sturges 1994). One could argue that determining financial eligibility does not belong in the assessment phase because it is time consuming and can work against the development of a positive working alliance between care manager and client.

Years of training case managers has convinced this author that client outcomes are highly dependent not only on structural arrangements, adequate resourcing, and the skill levels of care managers, but also on their motivation and their morale. Their performance is strongly influenced by how well the organisational environment takes account of their needs as well as the needs of clients.

Models of practice

There have been so many kinds of case management models in the USA that some have asked whether it is a distinct mode of practice after all (Rothman 1992). These models have varied both between and among different population groups of clients. Much has been learned through trial and error, particularly in the mental health field which is now using more intensive, clinically sophisticated, and multi-disciplinary models than in the past. The assertive community treatment approach in mental health (Witheridge 1992) uses an intensive outreach and clinical model which has been quite effective for targeted clients.

In long term care, the clinical aspects have been neglected, but at least there is more emphasis now on using multi-disciplinary teams. ACCESS in Rochester, New York, has adapted some of the features of the PSSRU models, with excellent outcomes for older people, including cost savings in rehospitalisation (Eggert *et al.* 1990). Improved outcomes in both mental health and long term care are correlated with access to and control over resources, frequent face-to-face contacts, lower case loads, long-term relationships between case managers and clients, and the successful integration of formal and informal supports. They reflect the understanding that many of the aspects of earlier practice did not work very well (Feiner 1994).

It would be impossible to describe the whole range of models that have been used in the USA, so what follows describes categories or types which are relevant at this time for the UK.

The stand alone versus the team model

Unlike the UK where most practice is done in teams, the case manager in the USA has been more likely to work alone. Particularly in long term care, case managers may be outstationed and meet infrequently with others doing the same kind of job. This has advantages in terms of developing independent practice and having autonomy, but has the disadvantages of providing much less support and learning because of lack of contact with peers and in some cases supervisors. In mental health, the team approach is much more common and on some teams caseloads are held by all rather than by the individual, or are mixed. Overall, the team approach commonly used in the UK is probably a better way to structure practice.

The broker versus the service manager

The broker model is where the case manager refers clients for needed services but does not have the power to purchase them. In contrast, the service management model gives budgetary control to the case manager (Applebaum and Austin 1990). Results from the evaluation of the large Channeling Demonstrations (Kemper 1988) compared outcomes for these two models. Services were more reliably delivered when the case managers could purchase them, but brokers had more frequent face-to-face contacts with clients. This suggests that the purchasing function requires more desk work. Since the service manager model is the one which the UK is implementing, a case could be made for increased clerical support for care managers.

The generalist versus the specialist model

The generalist model where social workers may work on a team which serves a range of types of vulnerable adults is not used in the USA. This is due in part to the separation of systems of care, and in part to the belief that case managers should be specialists in work with one group. Therefore case managers will be specialists in work with older people, with the severely mentally ill, and the like. Even in smaller towns and rural areas the specialist focus is maintained, but this also means that there may be less help available in these areas.

The issue of specialist versus generalist care management teams in the UK reflects the nature of the geographic areas served, the philosophy of a local authority, and the debate in social work over specialist versus generalist practice. In urban areas it is hard to find a rational explanation for using generalist teams. Research in the USA has demonstrated that working effectively over time with complex client disorders requires a substantive knowledge base which case managers cannot reasonably be expected to have about all groups of vulnerable adults (Rose 1992). Social work education is moving more toward specialisation, and this trend should strengthen care management practice (Hugman 1994).

Multi-disciplinary versus same discipline teams

Multi-disciplinary work in case management is more common now than it used to be. Often the nature of the client population determines whether this model is used. In work with frail and/or mentally ill older people it has been an advantage to have medical as well as social work personnel on a team since physical, cognitive, and psychological disorders are often so strongly intertwined. The disadvantage is that if a medical model predominates, social care can be diminished, and all problems reduced to medical ones (Estes and Binney 1991, Azzarto 1992). In mental health work, the team is often composed of social workers, nurses, psychologists and psychiatrists.

Multi-disciplinary models have many advantages, especially in terms of the resources and support they provide for both case managers and clients, but working relationships can be difficult. Research has shown that it takes some time for staff to understand each others' roles and the overlap between them (Øvretveit 1993, Sturges 1994). Until a team is functioning smoothly, it is counter-indicated to have too many cases or to involve clients and families in staffing. Specialised training is required for care managers on multi-disciplinary teams.

The UK has good reasons to use this model both because of the needs of vulnerable adults, and also because of the need to develop better working relationships between social services and the health service. The UK has some excellent models of multi-disciplinary teams from which the USA could learn. The dementia care teams, for example, composed of social workers, nurses and home care workers are quite innovative (Sturges 1992) as is the assignment of care managers to general practitioner (GP) practices. The latter model is not without its problems, however. It is important to use social workers as care managers in GP practices; if nurses do it then the medical perspective can predominate and social care will suffer. Supervision can also be problematical if the physician attempts to exert too much control over the care manager. GPs have more to learn about what care management is; many are not yet familiar or comfortable with needs led assessments and the focus on such concepts as user choice and empowerment (Henwood 1994).

Clients/families as case managers

One of the most interesting case management experiments in the USA was an effort in Boston to train families to do case management with their frail older relatives (Seltzer, Ivry and Litchfield 1987). The results were encouraging. Experiments in the UK in training younger disabled people to be their own care managers are also valuable. This type of model needs further elaboration but for those able to take more control of their lives, it is very promising. On the other hand, such models may be counter-indicated for some groups such as the very frail elderly who often require a good deal of support from a care manager.

Conclusion

The implementation of care management in the UK is a large scale and complicated undertaking which will take years to work out. Innovative model projects which pre-dated implementation have given way to the mainstreaming of care management throughout the country. There is presently some confusion about what care management is and how best to provide it as well as serious resourcing issues (Community Care 1995). Research in Scotland suggests that many local authority social work managers do not yet understand long term work with vulnerable adults and therefore do not know how to plan systems which promote continuity of care (Bland and Hudson 1994, Stalker, Taylor and Petch 1994, Sturges 1994).

Screening and assessment are frequently confused and needs led assessment is still not consistently practised despite all the rhetoric. These confusions reflect the fact that even though there are new labels, there is still a lot of old and not particularly functional practice going on. This is not surprising given the newness of case management and the description of it in government guidance. Conceptual clarification and skills training is badly needed: unfortunately, there are not enough experienced professionals in the country who have done this kind of practice and are also expert in designing and delivering relevant training. Universities and colleges must also educate their students for care management practice, but lecturers frequently are not experienced in how to do so. Therefore, training for those currently in practice and education for students entering it are quite underdeveloped.

Professional training, however, is not the only thing that is required. Care management will succeed in the UK to the degree that resourcing is available, national expectations are realistic, care managers are supported by organisations, and structural arrangements especially with the Health Service are satisfactory.

Community care in the USA has not been found to be particularly cost effective (Weissert 1985, Kemper, Applebaum and Harrigan 1987). Institutionalisation or re-hospitalisation may be cut back, but savings in these areas have been found to be off-set by increased demand for community based services, and by the costs of care management itself. Recent events in the UK show the same trends (Community Care 1995). As Kemper *et al.* (1987) said, 'policy makers should move beyond asking whether expanding community care will reduce costs to addressing how much community care society is willing to pay for, who should receive it, and how it can be delivered efficiently' (p.87).

Expecting care managers significantly to reduce the costs of community care is not realistic or fair; expecting them to be accountable, and to improve the quality of their clients' lives is. A major finding in both the PSSRU and Channeling demonstrations was that the well being of both users and carers was improved through community care. That, then, is a realistic goal and is justification enough for providing it.

What has been learned in the USA through the years has much to offer the UK, just as the USA has things to learn from the UK. The threat for the UK is that because the undertaking is so comprehensive, it will settle for administrative care management, when the research in the USA now points the other way. As Challis *et al.* (1990) has warned:

> 'The great danger of the administrative model is how easily it fits into existing structures and patterns of service provision, permitting an unnecessary and undesirable separation of responses to the practical needs of individuals from their psychological needs. It is possible that organizations, desiring minimal change as a result of the White Paper, would be attracted to the administrative model since it differs least from the existing forms of organization...' (p.161)

The author's research in Scotland saw definite movement towards the administrative model by many managers (Sturges 1994). Perhaps an advantage of the slow and sporadic developments in case management in the USA has been that at least there has been time to learn from mistakes. With the much more rapid implementation of care management in the UK, mistakes made at the beginning tend to become institutionalised, and therefore may be more difficult to correct in the long run. As Feiner (1994) has said about work with the severely mentally ill:

> 'Initial efforts to make this function simply a cost-saving, brokering device are now being seen as having failed, as the need for more sophisticated, therapeutically knowledgeable, interpersonally skilled case management is being advocated. The complexities of the illnesses and level of understanding necessary to deal with them are beginning once again to receive respect.' (p.22)

It is unfortunate that this level of understanding has not yet been reached by those who develop case management systems for older people in the USA.

The administrative model has the following characteristics: (1) A routinised way of working with people where assessments are formal, care plans are unimaginative, and monitoring is often by telephone rather than in person. (2) Case loads are large and the focus is on how many clients a case manager can see rather than on client outcomes. (3) There are too many forms for everything and workers feed the needs of computers, rather than information systems being designed to support care managers' work. (4) Tasks are split and provided by different workers rather than by one care manager over time. Therefore, local authorities hire assessors, care managers, and reviewers rather than investing these functions in one professional. These practices result in the deskilling of qualified social workers. (5) Emphasis is on providing formal services rather than on interweaving informal and formal care. Therefore, resource development in local communities is neglected. (6) Counselling is discouraged and care managers, who must do it, have to disguise it in their recording.

These negative practices have existed and still exist in the USA, although certainly not universally. There has been much less inclination, however, to split functions; this is a unique and particularly dysfunctional aspect of care management in the UK. The administrative model undermines morale, stifles flexibility and creativity, and leads to multiple assessments: thus outcomes for users and carers are negatively affected. We have empirical data about the results of these practices in the USA and studies have been cited throughout this chapter. The USA is still learning these lessons the hard way, and particularly in case management with older people has further to go. It is to be hoped that it won't take the UK twenty years to do so; however current trends are not encouraging.

The best hope for the UK is to look to the USA for lessons in what to avoid as well as for what to change, and to revisit its own innovative and effective pre-implementation models. The PSSRU models have much to offer current practice. They were based on a sophisticated understanding of case management world wide. As such, they incorporated what was best, avoided the worst, and added their own distinctive British stamp. The practices which they and other early and effective care management projects represented should not be lost.

Acknowledgement

I am grateful to Dr Peter Huxley for his comments on a draft of this chapter.

References

Applebaum, R. and Austin, C.D. (1990) *Long Term Case Management: Design and Evaluation*. New York: Springer.

Austin, C.D. (1990) 'Case management: Myths and realities.' *Families in Society*, 398–405.

Austin, C.D.(1992) When the whole is more than the sum of its parts: Case management issues from a systems perspective. Paper presented at The First International Conference on Long Term Care Case Management, Seattle, Washington.

Azzarto, J. (1992) 'Medicalization of the problems of the elderly.' In S. Rose (ed) *Case Management and Social Work Practice*. New York: Longman.

Bland, R. and Hudson, H. (1994) *EPIC: An Evaluation of a Multidisciplinary Care Management Project. Final Report*. Stirling: University of Stirling.

Boreland, A., McRae, J. and Lycan, C. (1989) 'Outcomes of five years of continuous intensive case management.' *Hospital and Community Psychiatry* 40, 4, 369–376.

Callahan, J.J. (1989) 'Case management for the elderly: A panacea?' *Journal of Aging and Social Policy* 1, 1/2, 181–195.

Cambridge, P. (1992) 'Case management in community services: Organizational responses.' *British Journal of Social Work* 22, 495–517.

Caragonne, P.(1981) *A Comparative Analysis of Twenty-two Settings Using Case Management Components*. Report of the Case Management Research Project. Austin, Texas.

Challis, D. (1989) 'Case management: problems and possibilities.' In I. Allen (ed) *Care Managers and Care Management*. London: Policy Studies Institute.

Challis, D., Chesterman, J., Traske, K., and Von Abendorff, R. (1990) 'Assessment and case management: Some cost implications.' *Social Work and Social Sciences Review 1*, 3, 1989–90, 147–162.

Challis, D. and Davies, B. (1986) *Case Management in Community Care*. Aldershot: Gower.

Community Care (1995) 'Department of Health acknowledges risks.' January 6–11.

Davies, B. (1992) *Care Management, Equity and Efficiency: The International Experience*. Canterbury: PSSRU, University of Kent at Canterbury.

Department of Health, Social Services Inspectorate and Scottish Office, Social Work Services Group (1991a) *Care Management and Assessment: Managers' Guide*. London: HMSO.

Department of Health, Social Services Inspectorate and Scottish Office, Social Work Services Group (1991b) *Care Management and Assessment: Practitioners' Guide*. London: HMSO.

Eggert, G.M., Friedman, B., and Zimmer, J.G. (1990) 'Models of intensive case management.' *Health Care of the Aged: Needs, Policies and Services 2*, 3, 357–372.

Eggert G.M., Zimmer, J.G., Hall, W.J. and Friedman, B. (1991) 'Case management: A randomized controlled study comparing a neighborhood team and centralized individual model.' *Health Services Research 26*, 471–508.

Estes, C. and Binney, E. (1991) 'The biomedicalization of aging: Dangers and dilemmas.' In M. Minkler and C.L. Estes (eds) *Critical Perspectives on Aging*. Amityville, New York: Baywood.

Feiner, J.S. (1994) 'Both ends of the river.' *Readings: A Journal of Reviews and Commentary in Mental Health 9*, 1, 20–23.

Fisher, M. (1991) 'Defining the practice content of care management.' *Social Work and Social Science Review 2*, 3, 1990–91, 204–230.

Franklin, J.L. (1988) 'Case management: A dissenting view.' *Hospital and Community Psychiatry 39*, 9, 921.

Henwood, M. (1994) *Fit for Change? Snapshots of the community care reforms one year on*. London: Nuffield Institute and Kings Fund Centre.

Hugman, R. (1994) 'Social work and case management in the UK.' *British Journal of Social Work 24*, 237–253.

Huxley, P. (1993) 'Case management and care management in community care.' *British Journal of Social Work 23*, 365–381.

Huxley, P. (1994) Personal correspondence.

Huxley, P.J. (1991) 'Effective case management for mentally ill people: The relevance of recent evidence from the USA for case management services in the United Kingdom.' *Social Work and Social Sciences Review 2*, 3, 192–203.

Intagliata, J. (1992) 'Improving the quality of community care for the chronically mentally disabled: The role of case management.' In S. Rose (ed) *Case Management and Social Work Practice*. New York: Longman.

Kane, R.A. (1992) 'Case management: Ethical pitfalls on the road to high quality managed care.' In S. Rose (ed) *Case Management and Social Work Practice*. New York: Longman.

Kane, R.L., Illston, L.H., and Millar, N.A. (1992) 'Qualitative analysis of the program of all-inclusive care for the elderly (PACE).' *The Gerontologist 32*, 6, 771–780.

Kanter, J. (1985) *Clinical Issues in Treating the Chronic Mentally Ill*. San Francisco, CA: Jossey-Bass.

Kemper, P. (1988) 'The evaluation of the national long term care demonstration. Overview of the findings.' *Health Services Research 23*, 1, 162–172.

Kemper, P., Applebaum, R., and Harrigan, M. (1987) 'Community care demonstrations: What have we learned?' *Health Care Financing Review 8*, 4, 87–100.

Kurtz, L.F., Bagarozzi, D.A. and Pollane, L.P.(1984) 'Case Management in Mental Health.' *Health and Social Work 9*, 3, 201–211.

Lamb, R.H. (1980) 'Therapist-case managers: More than brokers of service.' *Hospital and Community Psychiatry 31*, 762–764.

National Association of Social Workers (1992) *Standards for Case Management Practice*. Silver Spring, Maryland: National Association of Social Workers.

Øvretveit, J.(1993) *Coordinating Community Care: Multidisciplinary Teams and Care Management*. Buckingham: Open University Press.

Rapp, C.A. and Chamberlin, R. (1986) *Case Management with the Chronically Mentally Ill: The Results of Seven Replications*. Lawrence, Ks: School of Social Welfare.

Rose, S. (1992) *Case Management and Social Work Practice*. New York: Longman.

Rothman, J. (1991) 'A model of case management: Toward empirically based practice.' *Social Work 36*, 6, 520–528.

Rothman, J.(1992) *Guidelines for Case Management*. Itasca, Ill: Peacock.

Secord, L. (1987) *Private Case Management for Older Persons and their Families: Practice, Policy, Potential*. Excelsior, Minnesota: Interstudy.

Seltzer, M.M., Ivry, J. and Litchfield, L.C. (1987) 'Family members as case managers: Parnerships between the formal and informal support networks.' *The Gerontologist 27*, 722–728.

Stalker, K., Taylor, J. and Petch, A. (1994) *Implementing Community Care in Scotland: Early Snapshots*. Stirling: Social Work Research Centre, University of Stirling.

Steinberg, R. and Carter, G. (1983) *Case Management and the Elderly*. Lexington, Mass.: Lexington Books.

Sturges, P.J. (1985) *The Local Community as a Supportive Environment: Resource Redefinition for the Frail Elderly*. Unpublished doctoral dissertation, University of Washington, Seattle.

Sturges, P.J. (1986) *The Interdisciplinary Outreach Team: A New Service for the Community Hospital*. Fellowship Program in Applied Gerontology, Gerontological Society of America, Washington D.C.

Sturges, P.J.(1992) 'Comparing practice in the United States and the United Kingdom.' *Ageing International xix*, 3, 15–28.

Sturges, P.J. (1994) *The implementation of care management in Scotland: Comparisons with the US*. Paper presented at the 2nd Annual International Conference on Long Term Care Case Management, Toronto.

Weissert, W.G. (1985) 'Seven reasons why it is so difficult to make community-based long-term care cost-effective.' *Health Services Research 20*, 4, 424–433.

Witheridge, T.F. (1992) 'The assertive community treatment worker: An emerging role and its implications for professional training.' In S. Rose (ed) *Case Management and Social Work Practice*. New York: Longman.

Zadowski, R. and Eng, Z. (1988) 'Case management in capitated long-term care.' *Health Care Financing Review*, Annual Supplement, 75–81.

sment Process

Terry McLean

Introduction

Both before and after the implementation of the National Health Service and Community Care Act (1990) the issue related to community care which has perhaps received most attention within local authorities is that of assessment. There are a range of reasons for this. The Act specifically required local authority social services and social work departments to have their assessment arrangements in place by April 1993. Central government was critical of some of the ways in which social service staff had traditionally carried out assessments. Also the Social Services Inspectorate issued two documents (Department of Health, 1991a, b) containing comprehensive guidance which reflected the changes in assessment practice it wanted to have introduced.

Despite the fact that assessment is a central social work activity it is a process which has often been surrounded by confusion and controversy. Practitioners are sometimes unclear about the exact purpose of an assessment and may also have difficulty in defining the requisite skills needed to engage in the process effectively.

Sometimes health and social work staff have placed too much emphasis on assessing suitability for services which they may either control or be able to access. This service led style of assessment can make it less likely that services will be tailored to meet individual needs. It also encourages practitioners to engage in their own assessments rather than accept those carried out earlier by colleagues in the same department or belonging to other organisations. This can mean that users are subjected to multiple and sometimes unnecessary assessments. It is important, however, to realise that assessment is not an activity which is only carried out at the beginning of the contact with the user. Practitioners are required to assess any alteration in the user's need over time, and the appropriateness of the service response.

Criticism has been made of the relatively passive role traditionally played by users and carers within the assessment process. In recent years there has been considerable debate as to how to increase the influence users and carers have during assessments. Some local authorities have experimented with accepting the self-assessments of users. On occasion the needs of users and carers will conflict and increasingly departments are prepared to offer carers a separate assessment.

In an effort to improve the targeting of resources many local authorities have produced eligibility criteria which are used to determine which users are given access to an assessment and services. Another innovation designed to streamline the system is the introduction of different levels of assessment linked to the local authority's perception of the user's need at the stage of referral screening. In most if not all social services and social work departments a great deal of effort has gone into the design of assessment proformas. Either within these proformas or as a separate exercise some departments also use structured assessment instruments.

Assessment practice has seen considerable change in recent years. It is too early to make definitive statements about the value of the new approaches to assessment, but some early indications of the progress being made by local authorities do exist.

The purpose of assessment

Assessment is essentially about understanding and will normally take place within the context of a relationship between practitioner and user. The level of understanding gained by the practitioner will often reflect the quality of that relationship. Therefore the relationship-building skills of the practitioner are central to that process. The whole issue of assessment, however, is confused by the fact that the word is frequently used to describe a range of different purposes (Rowley and Taylor 1991). The practitioner will try to reach a consensus with the user with regard to needs and wants. The assessment of needs, however, has to be set against departmental policies on eligibility and cost. Obviously conflict can arise if users think that they have needs for services but the local authority considers that they are either not eligible for those services or that providing the care packages will be too expensive.

Frequently a key purpose is the assessment of risk. Stevenson and Parsloe (1993) distinguished between physical risk where a user is in danger of being harmed, social risk where a user may harm another, and emotional risk, where, for example, a carer's mental health may be damaged by the strains of their role. Getting an agreement on the nature and level of risk can be difficult. Elderly people sometimes place less emphasis on the importance of risk than their relatives and social workers (Neil 1989).

Assessment practice prior to the implementation of the National Health Service and Community Care Act 1990

A survey of four social services departments carried out by the Social Services Inspectorate (Department of Health 1991c) provided a useful insight into assessment practices prior to April 1993. Within the four departments assessment was not seen as a separate activity with a specific organisational requirement. No formal criteria for assessment existed and decisions about the level and type of assessment were largely service led.

To a large extent an assessment was provided for a service if individuals or referrers asked for it. If other social care needs emerged then additional assessments for other services would be undertaken. Individuals with multiple social care needs would receive multiple assessments.

In some of the specialist teams surveyed no assessment instruments existed. The content of assessment depended on the prevailing culture within those teams. The lack of assessment instruments caused difficulties when professionals were required to exchange information about users.

Quality standards had not been set for assessments. Departments relied instead on staff supervision and the professionalism of workers. Little evidence was found of genuine user or carer participation in the assessment process. Users and carers were not given a copy of assessment documents or asked if they agreed with them.

Permission to share the content of the assessment with other practitioners was not sought. Self-assessment by users or carers of their social care needs was rare.

Formal arrangements for interagency collaboration in assessment were also rare. There had been no development of interagency assessment tools. Different agencies frequently gathered the same information about the same user.

Databases were not shared between agencies. Other agencies tended to request services rather than assessments from social service departments. The social services departments were not inclined to trust the social care assessments undertaken by other agencies.

Other studies have made similar observations about traditional assessment practice. Beardshaw and Towell (1990) noted that assessment for home helps depended on informal rules and established routines rather than a clear policy regarding eligibility criteria. This approach can lead to poor targeting and therefore resources being spread too thinly.

A survey of hospital social workers by the Social Services Inspectorate (Department of Health 1993a) found that few users and carers were aware of having been assessed. They were rarely involved in multidisciplinary meetings and there was little evidence of formal written discharge plans. Ellis (1993) thought that some practitioners within her research sample made stereotyped responses to assessed need because of time and resource constraints. This caused them to make use of the limited range of resources to which they had easy access.

Practitioners' and managers' guides to care management and assessment

The National Health Service and Community Care Act (1990) gave local authorities the lead responsibility for coordinating the assessment of all community care needs. Central government explained how they wanted local authorities to carry out this responsibility in two guidance documents (Department of Health 1991a, b). These two documents have been extremely influential in shaping assessment practices within local authorities. This is evident from the assessment documentation produced by English social service departments which has been collated and circulated by the Department of Health's Community Care Support Force (1992).

Central to the concept of a purchaser-provider split is the belief that the interest of users and service providers sometimes conflict. Government took the view that it is therefore better to have different staff responsible for assessing need and organising packages of care, and for providing services. It is hoped that this separation will promote needs-led rather than service-led assessments, and that the care packages provided will be more likely to be tailored to individual needs.

This separation of assessment from service provision has enormous implications for the organisational structure of social services and social work departments, and for staff training. The guidance recognised that a clear purchaser-provider split will not always be possible. In particular it accepts that a counselling component may be incorporated within the assessment process and within other aspects of care management. If, however, the counselling needs of a particular user are substantial they should be provided by another practitioner.

Assessment staff will require a detailed understanding of the needs associated with particular user groups and a knowledge of the range of services and community resources available to meet those needs. In addition the guidance expects assessment staff to know their agencies' policies regarding eligibility criteria.

The guidance accepts that the assessment of need is a complex task. It defines need as 'the requirements of individuals to enable them to achieve, maintain or restore an acceptable level of social independence or quality of life as defined by the particular care agency or authority' (p.12). Need is therefore regarded as a dynamic concept which will vary with changes in national and local policy as well as with the availability of resources and patterns of local demand.

In the consideration of requests for help local authorities have to make decisions about the appropriate assessment response and priority level. The guidance suggests that the following factors should influence this decision making process:

- the severity or complexity of need
- the degree of risk or vulnerability of users and carers
- the level and duration of the projected resources required
- the degree of stress experienced by users, carers or other agencies
- the necessity for coordination with other care agencies, for example regarding hospital discharge or housing transfer
- the length of time already spent on a waiting list.

It is expected that the type of assessment response will usually be related to the level of presenting need except where a person is deemed to be disabled under the terms of the Disabled Persons (Services, Representation and Consultation) Act 1986. In such cases the local authority is required to offer a comprehensive assessment irrespective of the level of presented need.

If it appears that an individual has simple and well defined needs it is thought to be an inappropriate use of staff time and an imposition on the user to carry out a comprehensive assessment. Conversely if an individual has multiple needs it is inappropriate to do a brief and simple assessment.

To determine the appropriate level of assessment is an important and complex issue. The guidance offers a differentiated assessment system comprising six levels of assessment. The levels range from a simple assessment where an individual's needs are considered to be simple and well defined, to a comprehensive assessment where needs are ill defined, multiple and severe.

Obviously a situation may initially appear simple but if examined more closely may prove to be more complex. The guidelines encourage practitioners to be aware of indicators of more severe problems. To help in this task examples of trigger questions are offered.

The guidance also outlines the advantages and disadvantages of a range of organisational models in relation to the assessment task. This includes consideration of the relative merits of whether or not assessment is separate from purchasing and care planning. The advantages and disadvantages of not separating assessment from service provision are also outlined.

The health authorities are required to identify health care professionals to contribute to the local authority's assessment of care needs. Community nurses and general practitioners are expected to play a central role in the identification of social care needs. The local authorities may subcontract parts or all of the assessment process to other agencies but they retain legal responsibility for ensuring that specific standards of practice are met.

The guidance recognises that it is often difficult to separate the assessment of health and social care needs. The respective authorities are therefore encouraged to collaborate in the production of referral and assessment proformas.

With regard to the quality control of the assessment process, a range of quality standards is offered. Local authorities are encouraged to measure the effectiveness of the assessment process and the numbers of users satisfied with the outcome of their assessment. The amount of time between the referral and assessment should be measured and an estimate made of the level of user involvement.

Eligibility criteria and levels of assessment

In many respects the encouragement contained within the guidance for the prioritization of levels of need, the production of eligibility criteria and differentiated assessment systems would seem to be sensible advice. It can, however be extremely difficult for departments to operationalise such a system effectively. Also the guidance does accept that practitioners may find it difficult to accommodate an individual's perceptions of need within a framework of organisationally defined needs. Staff will have the difficult task of explaining the system to potential users and refers and justify to individuals why their situation has been categorised in a particular way.

Senior officers within the two local authorities surveyed by Ellis (1993) were of the view that prioritisation criteria reflected an increased emphasis on meeting basic survival needs at the expense of quality of life needs. One of the specialist social work teams within the same survey resisted the use of formal criteria because they considered it reduced their ability to respond flexibly. Ellis was critical of the possibility that a comprehensive assessment may only be provided for those users considered eligible for care management.

Practitioners such as occupational therapists and home help organisers who traditionally have experienced a high level of demand for their services have frequently used explicit eligibility criteria. Some departments have eligibility criteria for care management and separate eligibility criteria for specific services. This can cause tensions and confusion. Only a fraction of occupational therapists and home help cases will be care managed. Providers can sometimes be in the difficult position of refusing a care manager's request for a service or alternatively feeling obliged to give the care managed case preferential treatment to the detriment of other non-care managed cases. One possible solution to this dilemma is to have one senior person screening all new requests for help.

As referred to earlier, the Department of Health's Community Care Support Force (1992) collated assessment documentation from a range of English social services departments. With regard to the prioritisation of need and production of differentiated assessment systems, departments have clearly been influenced by the official guidance. Few departments, however had chosen to have as many levels of assessment as suggested. Perhaps this was because senior officials had taken the view that such a system would be too complex to operationalise.

One department had produced detailed criteria for five levels of need linked to four separate levels of assessment. Other departments had devised less complex systems, with three levels of need and three levels of assessment being common. It remains to be seen whether or not these systems are workable and useful. Several departments had made explicit statements that only users with the highest level of need would receive services.

Morris (1993) is critical of a system where professionals assess need. She argues that criteria which define eligibility and level of resource entitlement should be laid down in legislation as is the case with social security and homelessness. She believes that if this were the case, a system of self-assessment could be widely adopted.

User and carer participation in the assessment process

The perception of the user as a consumer of services which underpins much of central government's guidance related to community care, and the considerable current influence of the principles of normalisation within UK social work practice, combine to give prominence to the issue of user and carer participation in the process of assessment and service delivery. Meaningful participation is often hampered by the user having limited information about possible solutions to their perceived needs. Some service users have low expectations of influencing a process which involves relating to local authority representatives. Users will participate in assessment more effectively if they are encouraged to do so and acquire trust in the practitioners. This can take considerable time. Stevenson and Parsloe (1993) stressed the importance of appropriate pacing of the assessment process. Practitioners, however, are often under pressure to complete assessments quickly and therefore users and carers are not always given sufficient time to learn how to exert influence on the process.

Biehal (1993) describes the use practitioners made of the practice model developed by the Social Work in Partnership research project (SWIP). This model encouraged users to express their own view of their needs through the negotiation of jointly constructed lists of problems. The problems identified by the users were recorded in their own words on shared record sheets. If the practitioner perceived additional problems they were also recorded but clearly attributed to the worker.

Biehal found that some practitioners considered that this approach was only suitable for straightforward cases where users were clear about what they needed and the solutions were simple. Conversely, practitioners were less willing to use this model if they thought that the user had emotional problems, conflicts with carers, or were at risk. On some occasions, even, when practitioners and users had jointly constructed a list of problem areas the practitioner ignored the user input particularly with regard to priority and instead concentrated on what the practitioner considered to be the most important.

Ellis (1993) surveyed the practitioners of two local authorities focusing on the extent to which users and carers participated in assessment. She found that of the range of professionals included in the survey only social workers appeared to posses a clear conceptual framework for processing the conflicting needs of users and carers. It could be argued that when the needs of users and carers conflict, practitioners are required to display a sophisticated range of counselling skills and perhaps social workers are equipped to do this because of the emphasis on counselling within their training.

The Department of Health guidance encourages the use of self-assessment forms. So far local authorities have made limited use of this approach. One of the occupational therapy teams included in the Ellis survey experimented with the use of self-assessment forms but was forced to abandon them after a short period. Occupational therapists had difficulty in using the self-assessment forms as a basis for a service response and considered that they frequently generated more questions than they answered.

Whatever the instrument used the attitudes and values of the practitioner are probably more important in ensuring that users and carers participate effectively in the assessment process. Morris (1994) argues that despite the current rhetoric about participation, much of current practice is still paternalistic in its nature.

Inter agency and multi-disciplinary assessments

The need for effective inter agency and multi-disciplinary assessment is obvious, but it is difficult to achieve. Stevenson (1991) argues that the current emphasis on internal markets and a mixed economy of care creates a climate of competition rather than encouraging the cooperation necessary for effective joint working. In her opinion the motivation to cooperate is increased by the anxiety of practitioners, as is frequently the case in child abuse cases, and a shared perception on the part of practitioners involved of mutual benefit.

There are many other problems associated with multi-disciplinary assessments. Often there is a lack of agreement about the purpose of assessment and the demarcation of roles and responsibilities is frequently poorly defined. Disagreement can exist as to when a multi-disciplinary assessment is required and also regarding who should invite other professionals to contribute. A particularly sensitive issue in the question of whether or not a practitioner should be free to decide how they carry out their contribution to the overall assessment.

Giving a care manager specific responsibility for coordinating multidisciplinary assessment addresses some of the above issues. At this stage, however, it is unclear to what extent care mangers will acquire sufficient authority to coordinate effectively the assessment contributions of colleagues, particularly if they belong to other agencies. Care managers also need to consider that the professional background of colleagues may influence their approach to the assessment process. The occupational therapists included in the survey by Petch *et al.* (1994) demonstrated a marked tendency to define the needs of elderly people in terms of aids and adaptations.

A range of studies has demonstrated the problems which arise when more than one practitioner is involved in the assessment process. Neil's (1989) survey of applications for elderly residential homes found a lack of integration between the medical, functional, and social assessments. In Sharma, Aldous and Robinson's (1994) study of older people the usual general practitioner and social work assessments for residential care were supplemented by a formal multi-disciplinary clinical assessment at a rehabilitation centre. In 79 per cent of the cases treatable medical conditions were discovered. Twenty-nine per cent of cases where the social workers had recommended residential care were judged to be more suitably placed elsewhere following the multi-disciplinary clinical assessment. This study would suggest that a multi-disciplinary team can sometimes be more effective than practitioners from different disciplines operating relatively independently from each other, in that the assessments obtained more often lead to an appropriate service outcome.

In some cases agencies have endeavoured to address the problem of the coordination of multi-disciplinary assessment by negotiating joint assessment arrangements which sometimes include shared eligibility criteria and assessment proformas. For example in one area the content of the legally required over-75 assessments carried out by members of the primary health care teams will be shared with local authority staff if appropriate, and if the users agree. If an elderly person is experiencing substantial difficulties an assessment will be carried out by either a care manager or district nurse using the same proforma. This sensible arrangement has potentially considerable workload implications for the district nurses. It also requires the local authority to trust the assessment skills of the health care staff as they are in a position to influence the nature and cost of the care packages subsequently provided by the local authority.

In many parts of the country there already exist community mental health and community mental handicap teams who carry out many of the functions normally associated with care management and in addition provide services. Therefore this organisational model does not fit neatly with a purchaser-provider split. Nevertheless McGrath (1993), who surveyed the Welsh community mental handicap teams, maintains that these multi-disciplinary teams were able to combine assessment, service delivery and service development in a way which provided responsive and flexible services. She also asserts that the approach of the teams was needs-led, encouraged user participation and provided local community based provision. This contradicts central government's belief that giving the same practitioners responsibility for assessment and service delivery is less likely to lead to a needs led approach.

Wistow (1993) argues that all providers have an important and legitimate role to play in the assessment process. He argues that since assessment has to be an integral part of domiciliary, residential and day care, purchasers should make use of these skills while retaining overall responsibility for coordinating the assessment. Wistow emphasises the inter-dependence of purchasers and providers within the assessment process.

Similarly Francis (1993) quotes a social services director's belief that providers should be involved in the second stage of assessment after the needs of the user have been at least partially defined by the purchaser. Francis also notes that some providers still insist in doing an assessment in a manner defined by themselves irrespective of the nature of the assessment previously carried out by the purchaser. Frequently, provider assessments are concerned with issues related to suitability. Clearly a tension can exist between the provider's wish to do their own assessment and the undesirability of the user being subjected to multiple assessments. Managing this tension will stretch the negotiating skills of the care manager.

Assessment tools

The most commonly used tool for assessment purposes within social services and social work departments is a structured assessment proforma. Over the years departments have expended a great deal of time and effort in designing these proformas. They vary enormously between departments both in length and content. Recently many departments have revised them, in particular to remove their service-led features.

The length of proformas is to some extent a product of their being used for a variety of purposes. Obviously they provide a picture of the user's situation but they are also sometimes computer coded and used to provide aggregated management information on a range of issues, including unmet need.

While Peck, Ritchie and Smith (1992) make the valid point that the aggregation of unmet need should play a vital role in influencing a department's purchasing strategy, recording details for management information purposes is sometimes seen by practitioners as not central to the assessment needs of their particular user. Some practitioners in the Stevenson and Parsloe (1993) survey were critical of the use of assessment proformas, preferring instead to stress the importance of the relationship between user and professional.

Similarly Petch *et al.* (1994) found that most care managers in her survey of Scottish care management projects considered that the use of assessment proformas did not improve their assessment skills. She also found that proformas which were not liked by practitioners tended not to be completed properly.

On the other hand Ellis (1993) argues that an over-reliance on informal methods can lead practitioners to make too much use of intuition and to becoming more prone to being influenced by moral judgements. She argues that unless needs are systematically checked there is a danger that the lack of obvious evidence is taken as proof that certain needs do not exist.

Ellis also maintains that it is easier to change a proforma than the attitudes and values of a practitioner. Unless practitioners believe that it is appropriate to share power with users little will change. The inclusion, however, of a separate section within proformas which records the views of users and carers provides at least some encouragement to professionals to increase the level of participation of users and carers in the assessment process. Within the Petch survey some care mangers completed their proformas with the users and on some occasions the forms were left with the users to be completed by themselves.

In order to ensure that a practitioner covers an appropriate range of areas the assessment proformas often contain checklists. Rowley and Taylor (1991) maintain that if checklists are to be used they should clearly distinguish between an individual's incapacity and constraints within the environment. They should also address social and emotional issues as well as focusing on self care and daily living. In addition check lists should identify the areas in which the user requires assistance rather than containing a list of specific services such as meals on wheels.

As well as wide ranging proformas some departments use structured assessment instruments which measure specific attributes, the most common of which is dependency. There are many issues which require careful consideration associated with the use of dependency measures. Dependency is a highly complex concept and is therefore difficult to define. Dependency has numerous dimensions but most measures only include activities of daily living such as dressing, although some also address the issue of orientation, for example, whether or not a resident is able to find their bedroom. It is important to note that most measures fail to address the causes and sources of dependency. An individual with learning difficulties may be highly dependent not because of the nature of their disability but as a result of parental attitudes. At the assessment stage it is often important to discern cause as it may influence choices with regard to intervention.

There is sometimes an implicit assumption within the scoring system of the dependency measures that dependency is a one-dimensional attribute which can be described as a continuum ranging from completely dependent to completely independent. The aggregation of scores, however, which stem usually from descriptions of a wide range of behaviours can produce a simplistic and misleading picture of an individual's capabilities. Most dependency measures use an ordinal scale of measurement, which means that a score of ten reflects a higher level of dependency than of a score of five but not necessarily twice the level of dependency. With such a relatively unsophisticated scale of measurement great caution is required in the attribution of meaning to specific scores.

An example of a dependency measure is the Crighton Royal Behavioural Rating Scale (CRBS) which was originally devised for use within psychogeriatric hospitals. The items included focus on dependency on others for mobility and self care as well as reflecting aspects of mental impairment or disturbed behaviour. Wilkin and Thompson (1989) take the view that the CRBS is useful for providing an estimate of the level of dependency and confusion within the populations of residential homes and long stay hospitals but that it is not sufficiently sensitive to be used for individual assessment.

The Clifton Assessment Procedures for Elderly (CAPE) scale is widely used and consists of two separate schedules designed to measure cognitive performance and behavioural competence. The behavioural rating scale consists of eighteen items related to dependency and the scores are banded into five levels, with a grade of A reflecting a level of independence comparable to those living in the community without support and a grade of E reflecting maximum dependency which is a level most often seen within psychogeriatric wards. Although the CAPE was developed for institutional settings it is also sometimes used in domiciliary assessments. Wilkin and Thompson (1989), however, argue that the lack of items related to independent living limits its usefulness for the assessment of individuals within their own homes.

Wilkin and Thompson (1989) conclude that the information gained from the use of dependency measures either at an individual or group level can help in decision making but the measurement is not very precise and should therefore always be used in conjunction with other information. Also the measures tend to cover only limited aspects of every day life and they do not directly measure need for services. Finally, the use of dependency measures does not normally facilitate the participation of users in the assessment process.

A significant contrast to the use of dependency measures is the Getting to Know You Assessment Model designed by Brost and Johnson (1982). This approach is critical of the use of measurement techniques and gives central importance to the participation of the user. The value base of this assessment model is closely linked to the principles of normalisation. Although the model has been used with a range of user groups it was initially designed for use with individuals who have learning difficulties.

This approach advocates that an attempt should be made to interact with the user in a variety of settings. Significant carers and professionals should also be interviewed. The purpose of the assessment process is to complete a life story which addresses five basic questions:

- What is this person like?
- What has life been like in the past?
- What is life like now?
- In what ways does this person's disabilities complicate things?
- In what ways does it seem that life could change for the better for this person?

This comprehensive approach to assessment, whilst striving to capture the uniqueness of the individual user, can also prove to be highly time consuming.

A somewhat similar approach to assessment was designed by Seed and Kaye (1994). The Pitlochry Assessment Model was influenced by Seed's research on 41 service users in different settings who were being assessed for a possible move. He found that the different practices and attitudes of the professionals involved could be delineated into three assessment approaches. The readiness approach endeavours to assess the individual's level of disability and dependency with a view to deciding whether or not the person is ready to move to an alternative setting where more or less support is available. The suitability approach is an assessment for reception into a new setting. Not surprisingly some users were subjected to both readiness and suitability assessments. Seed found that a positive outcome for users was more likely if instead of focusing on readiness or suitability an opportunities approach to assessment was used. This assessment style is needs-led and emphasises the potential of the user. It focuses on the need for support rather than performance. The basis of assessment is the user's quality of life rather than definitions of dependency or suitability.

With reference to the work of Shalock (1989), three quality of life criteria were defined by Seed:

- environmental control addresses issues such as who decides when the user gets up and goes to bed?

- community involvement includes questions about work, transport and use of recreational activities.

- social relations focuses on friends, neighbours etc.

The Pitlochry assessment model incorporates the exploration of opportunities based on the above quality of life criteria. As part of the information gathering process, users and support workers are asked to keep diaries. Central to this assessment model is the belief that assessments should be an exploration rather than a test.

Assessment practice since the implementation of NHS and Community Care Act 1990

In the short time since the implementation of the NHS and Community Care Act several surveys have focused on social services and social work departments' assessment arrangements. The Department of Health Social Service Inspectorate (1993b) surveyed assessment and care management practices with regard to elderly and disabled people within six English social services departments. The survey found that eligibility criteria, whether for assessment or service provision, were not universally available. The written guidelines for staff lacked clarity and frequently needed early revision.

Some staff resisted the use of the new assessment proformas because they considered them to be cumbersome and repetitive, with their design being over influenced by the demands of information technology. Common referral systems across agencies were found to be rare and referrals from other agencies tended to be service-led rather than led by a request for an assessment.

The shift to a needs-led culture within departments was thought to be most marked where there was a definite purchaser-provider split with assessment clearly identified as an activity separate from service provision. This process was also facilitated by the existence of succinct and focused documentation. Most of the departments surveyed had developed four levels of assessment.

Staff responsible for allocating referrals to the appropriate level of assessment had little difficulty with the top and bottom levels but were less certain about when to allocate for a middle range assessment. This may suggest despite the advice contained within the guidance on this issue, that a differentiated assessment system containing several levels may be too complex to operationalise effectively.

The survey found that departments were moving towards establishing response times for completing assessments but they were not always met or published. The researchers found little development of the recording and aggregation of information from assessment with regard to unmet need.

The Social Work Services Inspectorate (Scottish Office 1994) interviewed practitioners and senior officers with responsibility for community care within all the Scottish social work departments. As with the Social Services Inspectorate study, the focus was on the implementation of the new community care arrangements for assessment and care management. This report concluded that it was too soon to be certain that the quality of assessment had improved but a range of positive indicators were detected. The assessment process had become more formalised within social work departments and there was found to be a better focus on the needs of vulnerable people. Some practitioners, however, found the assessment process lengthy and bureaucratic.

A much greater involvement in the assessment process of users and carers was reported. This included more verbal and written information regarding the assessment process being given to users and carers. The study also welcomed the development within some departments of user advocacy schemes designed to provide support for users and carers who had difficulty expressing their wishes. An improved assessment of carers' needs had led to an increased demand for respite care. The criteria for eligibility, however, were not well established or published and staff in some departments questioned their usefulness.

Departments were devoting more resources to assessing the needs of individuals who had either physical disabilities, learning difficulties or suffered from dementia. But there was some evidence that finding the time to adopt a needs-led approach to the assessment of older people was proving more difficult because of the volume of referrals. Concern was expressed that within several departments there appeared to have been little improvement in the assessment of individuals who have mental health problems.

Variable progress in establishing needs-led arrangements was reported. In some departments specialist services such as occupational therapy and home help were still receiving direct referrals rather than a single gateway for screening having been established. Only two departments regarded care management to be a separate job. The coordination of assessment was normally the responsibility of social workers and occupational therapists although some home help organisers were also given this task. In six departments responsibility for the coordination of assessment was sometimes delegated to health care staff, usually district nurses. In one authority general practitioners were allowed to coordinate assessments.

Where nursing home care was being considered the medical contribution to the assessment was usually provided by general practitioners; one department, however, used a consultant geriatrician. In three local authorities the information provided by medical staff was often considered inadequate and therefore caused delays in concluding the assessment.

A similar study was carried out by Stalker, Taylor and Petch (1994). The study was designed to assess the initial progress achieved by Scottish social work departments and health boards in the implementation of community care, including arrangements for assessment. Interviews were carried out with staff nominated by the agencies as having lead responsibility in the area of community care.

Despite the anticipation contained in the guidance that the numbers of hospital based social workers would increase due to their greater involvement in the assessment and discharge planning of patients, the Stalker study found the reverse. A definite trend was detected towards reducing the numbers of hospital based social workers, even involving the withdrawal of whole teams. To an increasing extent cover was being provided by community based social workers. Most health boards expressed concern about the adequacy of existing arrangements and the planned changes to the staffing levels of hospital social workers.

As with the Social Work Services Inspectorate study, Stalker found that none of the Scottish departments had followed the advice of the guidance to adopt six levels of assessment. Departments varied from one to four levels, with most adopting two. The words used to describe the different assessment levels varied, but the terms simple or limited are often used where needs appeared straightforward or where it is fairly clear that one service is all that is required. Where this is not the case the terms comprehensive or complex are used to describe the assessment process.

Where criteria existed for determining the level of assessment they were often broadly defined, frequently referring to degrees of vulnerability or complexity. Departments appeared anxious to avoid a rigid or mechanistic system with regard to the classification of assessment. One department had opted for a single level of assessment because it wanted staff to take as wide a view as possible when assessing the circumstances of users. Also they did not want to restrict the opportunities for staff to exercise their professional judgement.

The Stalker study noted that only two departments had so far created care management posts. Most departments, however, had not separated assessment from other care management functions, thereby ensuring the continuity of one practitioner, often a social worker, throughout the whole care management process. Stalker questions the ability of staff using this care management model to maintain a needs-led focus when doing an assessment and to avoid being influenced by their knowledge of the availability and costs of resources. Clearly this danger is increased if the practitioner is responsible for managing a budget. So far this would not appear to be a major issue as most front line staff have not yet been given budgetary responsibility.

Conclusions

There is widespread acceptance that in the past many users were subjected to poorly coordinated, often multiple, service-led assessments. It is now likely that most practitioners accept the importance of effective user and carer participation in the assessment process. There is, however, often still a gap between the rhetoric associated with participation and the paternalistic nature of some practice. Clearly, a major positive development has been the shift from a service-led to a needs-led approach.

This welcome change could, as is claimed by the Social Services Inspectorate survey (Department of Health 1993b), be attributed to the emergence of a purchaser-provider split within local authorities, but it is too early to be certain about this. Even if this were the case the question remains as to whether or not the improvement in assessment practice and increased tailoring of care packages is worth the considerable organisational upheaval and strain on relationships between practitioners.

An alternative and currently less fashionable view would be that the benefits for the user from a purchaser-provider split are not worth the organisational dislocation and that it is more effective to combine assessment, service delivery and service development as already happens within community mental handicap teams and resource centres for elderly people. Within this scenario the development of independent advocacy schemes might ensure that the interests of providers do not prevail over those of users where conflicts exist.

Assessment proformas take a long time to design and sometimes a long time to complete. The extent to which they improve the quality of assessments is uncertain. Some proformas are criticised by practitioners for being too long to be helpful. A clear separation of details which are helpful to those, including the user, who are directly involved in the assessment process from facts which are required for management information purposes might improve the situation. It would appear that specific assessment instruments are used to some extent within residential homes and hospitals but have less influence within domiciliary settings.

The enthusiasm reflected in the Social Services Inspectorate guidance for the prioritisation of need, eligibility criteria and the development of levels of assessment has had a substantial influence within many local authorities. At this stage it is too early to judge whether these developments ensure a more effective targeting of an appropriate assessment response or unnecessarily over complicate and bureaucratise the assessment process.

Finally, with regard to inter agency and multi-disciplinary issues there are a number of interesting innovations involving the shared development of referral forms and assessment proformas. Also in some instances sufficient trust has been established for local authorities to subcontract their assessment role to professionals within other agencies. Currently, however, these examples are not widespread and there is a pressing need for much greater progress on this issue.

References

Beardshaw, V. and Towell, D. (1990) *Assessment and Case Management. Implications for the Implementation of 'Caring for People'*. London: King's Fund Institute.

Biehal, N. (1993) '"Changing Practice": Participation, rights and community care.' *British Journal of Social Work 23*, 443–458.

Brost, M. and Johnson, T. (1982) *Getting to Know You*. Wisconsin, USA: New Concepts for the Handicapped Foundation Inc.

Department of Health, Social Services Inspectorate (1991a) *Care Management and Assessment: Practitioner's Guide*. London: HMSO.

Department of Health, Social Services Inspectorate (1991b) *Care Management and Assessment: Managers' Guide*. London: HMSO.

Department of Health, Social Services Inspectorate (1991c) *Assessment Systems and Community Care*. London: HMSO.

Department of Health, Community Care Support Force (1992) *Assessment of Need: Support Force Information Pack*. Unpublished.

Department of Health, Social Services Inspectorate (1993a) *Social Services For Hospital Patients III: The user and carer perspective*. London: Department of Health.

Department of Health, Social Services Inspectorate (1993b) *Inspection of Assessment and Care Management Arrangements in Social Services Departments: Interim Overview Report*. London: Department of Health.

Ellis, K. (1993) *Squaring the Circle. User and Carer Participation in Needs Assessment*. York: The Joseph Rowntree Foundation.

Francis, J. (1993) 'Shouldering the Burden.' *Community Care 994*, 24–25.

McGrath, M. (1993) 'Whatever happened to teamwork? Reflections on CMHTs.' *British Journal of Social Work 23*, 15–29.

Morris, D. (1994) 'Time to Come in From the Cold.' *Community Care 1010*, 18.

Morris, J. (1993) 'Criteria Motives.' *Community Care 949*, 17.

Neil, J. (1989) *Assessing Elderly People for Residential Care: A Practical Guide.* London: National Institute for Social Work.

Peck, E., Ritchie, P. and Smith, H. (1992) *Contracting and Case Management in Community Care: The Challenges for Local Authorities.* CCETSW Paper 32. London: Central Council for Education and Training in Social Work.

Petch, A., Stalker, K., Taylor, C. and Taylor, J. (1994) *Assessment and Care Management Pilot Projects in Scotland: An overview.* Stirling: Social Work Research Centre, University of Stirling.

Rowley, D. and Taylor, L. (1991) *Planning and Managing Community Care.* Dundee: Department of Social Work, University of Dundee.

Seed, P. and Kaye, G. (1994) *Handbook for Assessing and Managing Care in the Community.* London: Jessica Kingsley Publishers.

Shalock, R. (1989) 'Quality of life – its measurement and use.' In P. Seed and G. Kay (1994) *Handbook for Assessing and Managing Care in the Community.* London: Jessica Kingsley Publishers.

Sharma, S., Aldous, J. and Robinson, M. (1994) 'Assessing applicants for part three accommodation: is a formal clinical assessment worthwhile?' *Public Health 108,* 91–97.

Scottish Office, Social Work Services Inspectorate (1994) *Assessment and Care Management: Progress to Date.* Edinburgh: Scottish Office, Unpublished.

Stalker, K., Taylor. J., and Petch. A. (1994) *Implementing Community Care in Scotland: Early Snapshots.* Community Care in Scotland Discussion Paper No 4. Stirling: Social Work Research Centre, University of Stirling.

Stevenson, O. and Parsloe, P. (1993) *Community Care and Empowerment.* York: Joseph Rowntree Foundation.

Stevenson, O. (1991) *Care Management and Assessment: Designing the Picture for a Complicated Jigsaw.* Unpublished Conference Papers. Edinburgh: Scottish Office, Social Work Services Group.

Wilkin, D. and Thompson, C. (1989) *Users' Guide to Dependency Measures for Elderly People.* Social Services Monographs: Research and Practice. Sheffield: University of Sheffield.

Wistow, G. (1993) 'The Purchasing Dilemmas.' *Community Care 994,* 23.

Chapter 5

Care Management
A Manager's Perspective

Laura Bannerman and Bill Robertson

Introduction

A manager's perspective on care management might focus solely on the challenge of delivering what was characterised as the ideal in an article in *Community Care*:

> 'The care manager makes the assessment visit armed with a laptop computer on which is stored information about every community care resource available... They are listed and costed and the capital and revenue cost of each item is regularly updated... While matching the user's needs to what is available, the care manager is confident of four other functions which the briefcase-sized laptop can fulfil:
>
> - a rapid assessment of the user's income from all sources including benefit entitlement, and link them with the SSD's charging policy,
> - immediate details of the amount of money left in the care manager's budget,
> - it can feed the financial consequences of the assessment into an information system which provides senior management with an instant check on how the department's overall budget is performing; and,
> - it will log in dates of visits and deliveries of services for the care manager to monitor.' (Clode 1993, p.29)

This perspective, complicated and challenging as it is with regard to the development of appropriate assessment instruments and processes, resource data bases, unit costing, commitment accounting and devolved budgetary management and the specification of suitable information technology hardware and software, is based nevertheless on a limited view of care management. Managers must take account of a broader range of perspectives: professional, political, cultural and organisational.

Care management has become a shibboleth in some quarters, representing a process which threatens the ethos and values of social welfare, just as the 'mixed economy of care' is considered by many a euphemism for the privatisation of social care. The success of care management will depend not just on being able to solve the very real technical and logistical difficulties which it presents, but also on whether some new consensus on the welfare state can be reached. This consensus would have to include central and local government, health and social care agencies in the public and independent sectors and, most important, local communities and individuals with care needs.

There is wide support for the prospect of full user and carer participation in the assessment of individual needs, the development of flexible services to meet these needs, the promotion of real choice and the deinstitutionalisation of care for all but a few. The promotion of social welfare, however, should not involve leaving vulnerable individuals without support in the community, exploiting informal carers or dismantling public sector provision to drive down the wages of those working in the care sector to poverty levels.

The development of care management is, therefore, not only an important consideration for social work management but ultimately a vital public and political issue. In Scotland it is being undertaken within local authorities which by tradition and inclination are collectivist and committed to the public provision of welfare. As Midwinter (1993) comments in an article on local government reform:

> 'In the main, Scottish local politics reflect the traditional consensus in favour of municipal provision, whilst political conflict is fought over the scale of provision and the levels of local taxation.' (p.54)

This does not rest easily with the imperatives of some within central government who view the development of choice as being inextricably linked to the contraction of the public sector. The management of the changes brought about by the 'lead role' given to local authority social work departments for care in the community has been complicated by wider controversies on the future role of the National Health Service in continuing care; and the balance of responsibilities between the state and the individual, particularly in the care of older people.

This chapter explores issues which will be familiar to any social work manager involved in community care. It begins with a description of how care management was introduced in Tayside. It goes on to offer some comment and analysis on selected themes of assessment methods and staff roles, training and staff development, finance and information technology systems and performance measurement. It concludes with an assessment of where we think we have got to in Tayside and what we believe lies ahead for us in the future within a rapidly changing environment.

An overview of the introduction of care management in Tayside

Section 55 of the National Health Service and Community Care Act 1990 places a new duty on social work authorities to assess the needs of persons for whom they have a power, or are under a duty, to provide or secure the provision of community care services. Authorities must decide what services to provide, having regard to the results of the assessment.

Scottish Office Circular advice (Scottish Office 1991a) indicated that assessment should be set within a system of care management. Care management is described as:

> 'A process of relating services to individual needs. It is founded on a needs led approach to the provision of community care. It aims to respond appropriately to individual needs by enabling the consideration of a range of options and by making effective use of available resources through concentrating on those people who have the greatest need.' (p.3)

The circular went on to advise authorities that they should refine their existing arrangements for assessment in accordance with a needs-led approach, whilst progressively introducing tasks involved in care management within a supporting budgetary framework.

Serious preparation for the introduction of the statutory duty to assess need within a care management framework began in Tayside in 1991 when a series of recommendations concerning assessment procedures, care management processes, financial processes, resource information requirements and training were put to the senior management team of the social work department. This led to proposals for the development of pilot studies that would test out the practicalities of implementing care management.

Four large scale pilot projects were set up. Each covered a different geographical area; three were concerned with particular client groups and one covered all adult care client groups. The four projects covered respectively: the community care needs of all older people within the city of Perth (with approximately 7300 people over 65); the needs of adults with learning disabilities in Dundee (with approximately 560 people over 16 with learning disabilities); the needs of adults with physical disabilities in Dundee (with approximately 6000 adults under 60 with physical disabilities); and the needs of all the adult community care groups in the towns of Forfar and Kirriemuir (with a total population of approximately 28,000).

The pilot studies shared several characteristics. They were to test the usefulness of two assessment tools; care planning and assessment was to be undertaken by assessment/care management teams with a range of skills; they were to operate within the current social work resources; a budget would be allocated to each pilot; the manager of the pilot would be responsible for that budget; and more flexible forms of home care would be introduced, supported by social care officers who would be drawn from the existing home help service.

A multidisciplinary group with some service user involvement was set up under independent chairpersonship to oversee an evaluation of the pilot studies, with the expressed intention of using the experiences to inform the development of care management in the department. The authority's community care plan (Tayside Regional Council, 1992a) stated that the pilot studies would be used to assess:

- the models of service delivery in terms of value for money;
- client satisfaction;
- resource issues and workforce planning;
- the application of the assessment tool;
- whether the model put forward would meet central government objectives laid out in chapters one and ten of the White Paper;
- financial systems, arrangements for budgetary management and financial assessment;
- the application of the client index system (a Tayside computer based system of recording social work client data);

- measures of quality assurance;
- whether the process of assessment and care management could be combined with service provision;
- the response times to requests for service;
- the process of assembling and implementing care packages;
- the resource data base requirements;
- deficits in current services and infrastructure costs.

The multidisciplinary group met regularly during the period of the pilot studies and their findings were drawn together in a report prepared for the Social Work directorate (Tayside Regional Council 1992b).

The pilot studies thus became an important focus of attention within the department. This was partly because of the sheer scale of the social work activity involved, partly because there was a tacit acceptance that introducing arrangements for care management would have a profound effect upon the organisation and delivery of services, and partly because of the central role seen for care management in the development of central government community care policy. The third of the government's six key objectives for service delivery laid out in the White Paper (Caring for People 1989), 'to make proper assessment of need and good care management the cornerstone of high quality care' was often quoted at that time. There was a general concern that there was limited documented information about the operation of care management in the UK. The operational managers with the responsibility for developing care management in their areas drew heavily on the care management guidance for practitioners and managers prepared by the Department of Health (Department of Health 1991a, 1991b) and reports on the Kent Community Care Project (Davies and Challis 1986, Challis and Davies 1986) and the Gateshead Community Care Scheme (Challis *et al.* 1990). The scale of the operation meant that the managers had to be given the flexibility to develop and adjust their approach according to experience gained and local circumstances.

Notwithstanding the flexibility and openness of the different pilot approaches, one fundamental principle was determined at an early stage. It was that assessment and care management as a combined function should be separated out from service provision. The statutory requirement introduced by the 1990 Act was to assess individual need rather than to introduce care management. The view was taken in Tayside, however, that assessment is an integral part of the process of care management, which includes the dissemination of information, the assessment of need, care planning, the implementation of the care plan, monitoring and review as described in Department of Health guidance (Department of Health 1991a, 1991b).

The department's main goal was the development of good assessment of need and responsive services provided within a devolved budgetary framework. The attractions of care management for the social work department were that it promised improvements in service. Assessment would be based upon need rather than led by the availability of services, and the different components of care management would be performed by a single practitioner with a clearly defined responsibility. These decisions were an important determinant of the organisational steps which followed and were taken within an overview of tasks and available resources.

In organisational terms, care management has resulted in most social workers and some occupational therapists working in adult care transferring to assessment and care management teams. The exceptions to this are the home help and occupational therapy services which retain integrated assessment and provider functions. There are also two community care teams, for people with addictions and those who are HIV positive or have AIDS, which combine functions of assessment and care provision. Care managers for people with mental illness have in practice continued to provide ongoing support and counselling which goes beyond care management and review.

Structural developments resulting from community care affected all areas of service provision. Thirty-one cost centres were established, including sixteen in community care, which integrate the responsibility for the assessment of individual need and care management. Assessment and care management are separated from service provision only in community care services. Cost centres are user group and geographically based, reflecting urban and rural variations. Each cost centre has a manager with overall responsibility for assessment of individual need and care management, the budget for the user group or area, physical resources, human resources, local purchasing and contracting, standards and quality assurance, cost centre information technology, local area networks and management information.

The approach and structure which is being adopted in Tayside aligns most closely to the description of local purchaser/commissioner and provider separation as outlined in the Department of Health publication on Purchaser/Commissioner and Provider Roles (Department of Health 1991c). The perceived strength of this model is that a clear purchaser/commissioner and provider split at local level, and a combination of roles under care management, facilitate responsiveness. The corresponding weakness is that it 'lacks obvious focus for strategic planning in relation to in-house provider roles' and 'requires operational middle managers to balance interests of purchasers/commissioners and providers' (Department of Health 1991c, p.29).

In reality, however, there is a strategic framework for the planning and commissioning of services and the development of contracts for social care which set out clear parameters for the range, standards and mix of care services which should be procured or provided within a budget which is allocated according to a needs analysis.

The centre retains a strong hold on policy direction and resourcing as well as central commissioning of in-house and some external provision. Devolved management is about flexibility, responsiveness and the most effective use of resources within which local commissioning has a role to play. No large scale organisation, especially within the public sector, can or should conform to a perfect model. Tayside's model will continue to adapt and evolve within the key objective of providing good quality responsive services, not on the basis of rigid adherence to some ideal of purchaser/provider purity.

If local authorities are directed to introduce high level splits between commissioner and provider roles, then mechanisms will have to be established which ensure that quality, flexibility and responsiveness are maintained. These are, however, certain to be expensive to implement.

Some themes and issues arising from the introduction of care management

Assessment methods and staff roles

The decision to separate out care management from service provision led to the organisational changes outlined above. It also immediately created a focus for the care management activity which brought with it inevitable questions about the roles, tasks and the professional development of staff working as care managers. During the process of the development of the pilot studies, the assessment instruments became the focus of social workers', occupational therapists' and community nurses' concerns surrounding the change of role that came with the introduction of care management.

Two instruments were in use at the beginning of the pilot studies, one which was developed jointly with health board professionals for use with people with learning disabilities and another which emerged through a process of refinement of assessment documentation that had been current in the social work department at the time of the establishment of the pilot projects. Assistance was sought from Stirling University to evaluate the assessment instruments (Social Work Research Centre 1994). A revised instrument was designed by those working in the pilot study and community nursing staff. It was adopted as the format for future assessment along with supporting care management documentation. It is also incorporated into a practice manual for use by care management and other staff (Tayside Regional Council 1993) which is currently under review.

There were organisational, administrative and professional issues and tensions which developed around the assessment instrument. In reality, the instrument itself was a secondary issue. The primary issues related to the changing nature of the social work task, the social worker's role and relationships with other professions.

The issue of whether the role of the social worker is challenged positively or negatively by care management is posed by Harvey and Philpot (1993). They conclude that:

> 'If more and more people are to be dealt with by care management, it is better that social workers embrace it enthusiastically. Then they will be there to use their skills and values to help meet needs and to fight for users' rights. It is the opportunity not the threat that social workers should recognise.' (pp.17–18)

In Tayside, community nurses, social workers and occupational therapists have been employed as care managers. Most have adopted the role enthusiastically, as Harvey and Philpot recommend. They all comment favourably on the lead role that the 1990 Act has given to social work, which provides a clear basis for negotiation and cooperation with other professionals, particularly health professionals. Care management has demonstrated the need to draw on a broad range of skills which includes assessment, care coordination, financial management, income maximisation, and commissioning and contracting. Most care managers would say their professional training has only partly equipped them for their new responsibilities. A need has been established for a more detailed knowledge and understanding of the aetiology and management of mental illness, learning disability and ageing.

Interagency relationships have been tested by the introduction of care management. It confers a more defined role on the social work department and the care manager and, in certain circumstances, it shifts power and authority. It is probably the shift in power which has led to some of the inter-professional tension which has accompanied the introduction of care management. Experience of care management in Tayside would suggest that proximity and frequent inter-agency contact help to ease these tensions and that this is important between those who are responsible both for assessment and service provision.

The functional separation between assessment and care management, and service delivery, has also challenged the organisation of resource provision. Care managers, who are encouraged to assess need rather than match people with existing services, are asking service providers for greater flexibility and variety in the services they provide. This is particularly so with home care. Day and residential care providers are also being encouraged to adapt and extend the choice of services they provide to meet needs on an individual basis and to demonstrate closer integration with their surrounding communities. Planners and managers of services are using aggregated assessment information when negotiating for resources, defining standards and specifying service requirements. The message is getting through, but just as the social worker role is being challenged by care management, well tried methods of delivery of direct care are also being challenged.

Training and staff development

Over the past two years, substantial investment has been made in Tayside as elsewhere in training covering care management; devolved budgetary management; training for middle managers; volume training for residential, day care and domiciliary care staff; and management development training for front line supervisors and managers.

Whilst the endeavour and achievements so far have been impressive, there has been a lack of coherence in the training which has been provided. The skills, competencies, values and knowledge which are required within social care, social work and management require to be set out within a comprehensive national framework of training and recognised awards. This has not as yet been established and much improvisation has been required between social work training sections and educational establishments to ensure that staff within the department and within the private and voluntary sectors are prepared for implementation of care in the community. In particular, it must be acknowledged that no satisfactory training exists in assessment and care management skills. What has been provided so far in Tayside is far short of what is required.

The rules and requirements for the award of the Diploma in Social Work contained in CCETSW's Paper 30 (CCETSW 1994) are currently under review. The Care Sector Consortium (the Occupational Standards Council for Health and Social Care) is also undertaking two major projects which relate the review of the DipSW and the development of a framework of Occupational Standards. These are the Functional Mapping Projects, which will cover the entire health and social care sectors, and the Social Care Project, which will develop standards for a range of functions, particularly in relation to new community care roles.

Social work managers are looking to these reviews to provide the required framework and continuum, not just for care in the community but also for children's services and services to the criminal justice system. The timetable for all of this work is tight and the intellectual and political challenges are considerable. There is, however, an emerging common appreciation of the need for a continuum of qualifications for all social work staff. How this continuum (or continua) is resourced is one of the challenges which must be faced along with the others which arise in implementing the new legislation.

Finance and information technology systems

Over the past period, Tayside, like many other social work departments, has moved steadily from a centralised model of service delivery based on service functions (residential care, fieldwork, etc.) to an integrated decentralised model with delegated financial control. The authority's corporate budgetary system has been a traditional incremental system which provided for changes around the margins. Budgets have been set by a process of negotiation and compromise with the negotiations, by and large, conducted at a corporate level with little or no involvement of accountable managers.

The first changes which have been introduced along with devolved budgets are new *virement* rules which give accountable managers more flexibility in the use of their budgets. A revised corporate financial system is also being introduced. It will provide managers with outline financial information which will record not only actual payments but also committed expenditure. A major weakness in the corporate financial system is that committed expenditure will not include internal staff costs. The system allows for budget profiling which will improve the ledger's usefulness as a managerial and planning tool. It will also provide for journal entries to adjust budgets based on the 'purchase' of services across cost centres.

The new ledger system as it relates to social work will be based on the new cost centre structure and the standard classification for social work outlined in Accounting for Social Services in Great Britain (CIPFA 1993). *Virement* adjustments will also be entered into the budget throughout the year and it is fully anticipated that accountable managers will have more relevant information on budgetary performance in future, albeit on an historic basis.

The corporate financial system cannot, however, provide detailed resource and activity information which would allow the integration of assessment, resource provision and budgetary performance. In essence, it cannot directly relate activity or expenditure to individual client need – thus the need for departmental informational technology systems.

Tayside, like other social work departments, is confronting the challenge of developing an integrated information technology system which meets departmental needs and relates appropriately to other corporate systems such as creditors, debtors, payroll and personnel systems. Any social work information technology strategy at present will probably require a framework which will accommodate change and extensions over a significant time span, the ability to help operational staff in their day-to-day tasks and the ability to produce management information (as a byproduct if possible). Social work managers are grappling with the concepts of 'open systems' and 'client server' architectures as well as local area and wide area networking. Whilst doing so they are acutely aware that no appropriate lead or resourcing for information technology developments for community care has been forthcoming from the Scottish Office.

The computer market has also been slow to come forward with products which meet the needs of social work authorities. Clode (1993) explored the reasons for this and concluded it 'was because of the complexity of the task, the substantial retrenchment by computer firms from the beginning of the recession and the justifiable caution of purchasers in being specific about future requirements' (p.31).

Tayside, having appraised several commercial proposals and products, has decided to go for an in-house development. The Social Work K2 project (our mountain to climb) will be based on a relational data base management system (Oracle V7). The overall objective of the project is to establish and integrate client and resource information systems that cover all areas of activity within the department.

Even when K2 is developed and operational, however, we will still not have a mechanism which translates committed packages of care based on unit costs directly into corporate financial systems. Accountable managers will require to compare corporate ledger information with aggregate information derived from expenditure attributed to each person on the department's Known Persons Index (a new client index system). The linking of these systems through 'actual expenditure' on a client basis will require time and resources which are unlikely to become available to Tayside Region.

Performance measurement

There is increasing attention being given within local government to 'performance' issues. This is particularly the case with care in the community where both the Wagner (1988) and Griffiths (1988) reports emphasised the importance of performance measurement. The inception of arms-length inspection units, the requirement to publish plans for care in the community (and other services) and the establishment of the Social Work Services Inspectorate with a role of inspecting, monitoring and evaluating local authorities' social work plans and services have all contributed to the emphasis on performance and quality.

The development of performance review and measurement within social work is also being influenced and directed by the provision of the Local Government Act 1992 relating to performance indicators and the role of the Accounts Commission in overseeing these and other financial management expectations.

There is growing awareness and appreciation among social work managers of the need for quality assurance systems within social work. Quality assurance systems have their origins in industry and are written in a language which often appears obscure and irrelevant to social work. Most social work managers would, however, relate to a system which sets out a mission for the whole organisation, service requirements with success criteria, a process for achieving requirements, systems for monitoring success or failure, systems of monitoring records, auditing processes and corrective action and reviewing systems' (Bone 1991). They would agree with the assertion made in the report prepared for the Department of Health by Kings Fund College (Department of Health 1992) that 'quality assurance initiatives can give impetus to innovation' and 'that the commitment to quality can be a powerful integrating device for managing change' (p.5). Our approach in Tayside involves setting down standards; developing management systems for assuring quality; the selection of performance indicators; developing management information; the integration of standards and performance indicators into plans, service specifications and contracts; setting occupational standards and training of staff and the publication of standards for users and carers. This process has generated a considerable workload. In particular, setting down standards is proving to be a painstaking and time consuming activity for which there is no short cut – it is a slog!

The development of management systems for assuring quality and measuring performance is in turn creating demands for management information of a kind not previously generated within social work departments. As was asserted in a special issue of the journal of the Social Services Research Group:

'As interest grows in "performance" so the deficiencies of current information on the work of the social services departments have become more apparent. Accounting data is by far the most extensive information on the work of departments, but is inadequately related to an increasingly complex pattern of services and staffing – "Quality Assurance" and "Performance Review" are increasingly making their appearance in management terminology in the public sector. Yet few initiatives of this type are coherently linked to the development of systems to generate performance data for managers.' (SSRG 1988, p.1)

In Tayside, these issues are being addressed with our in-house K2 Information Technology Project.

Reflections and conclusions

A year after the full implementation of the National Health Service and Community Care Act, 1990 and one year into the delivery of community care services with the benefit of care management we believe we have a solid basis for its development in Tayside. The concept of care management is embodied in professional, managerial and structural terms within the Social Work Department. This has involved considerable change and the prospect of local government reorganisation means that further change is likely. Since local government reorganisation self evidently will be accompanied by political as well as organisational change it will be important to hold on to the lessons that have been learned to date. If there is conflict between central and local government about the overall direction of social policy then clarity of purpose will be difficult to maintain.

Operationally, we have undertaken a review of care management, in particular its links with home care and occupational therapy services. This may well lead to the full integration of these services into existing care management teams and resource structures. Although this would be costly to implement, the view taken is that greater efficiency and effectiveness will outweigh additional costs. Increasingly, the timely and appropriate provision of home care and equipment is seen as the key to preventing unnecessary admissions to care or hospital, or facilitating appropriate discharges into the community. The bringing together of all assessment activity into one team in each cost centre would also allow the development of a coherent system of simple and complex assessments linked by consistent and standardised screening methods.

We are very conscious from our experience to date that the instruments and documentation that are used for care management have to be complementary to the process and not a hindrance to it. They will remain under continued review and be developed in close cooperation with the staff who use them.

Care management requires sophisticated information technology and financial systems. We are finding these time consuming to specify and expensive to implement. Getting them right involves a sustained dialogue between those involved in care management, those providing services to meet the needs identified and those designing and developing the systems.

Finally, with regard to the need for a new consensus for care in the community, it is to be hoped that Scotland is not about to enter a period of new controversy caused by the government going ahead with plans to force the privatisation agenda by requiring local authorities to spend fixed percentages of Department of Social Security transfer funds. This would represent a fundamental change in the mixed economy of care and would be likely to be opposed by Scottish local authorities. It would also create further concerns over the implications of local government reorganisation for care in the community.

A new consensus for care management therefore seems some way off. Management will have to operate within the tensions and upheavals which may arise over the next few years, and grapple with the issues of flexibility and responsiveness in the culture of contracts.

References

Bone, C. (1991) *Modern Quality Management*. London: Longman.

Caring for People: Community Care in the Next Decade and Beyond (1989). Cm 849. London: HMSO.

CCETSW (Central Council for Education and Training in Social Work) (1994). Press release 1 March 1994.

Challis, D. and Davies, B. (1986) *Case Management in Community Care*. Aldershot: Gower.

Challis, D., Chessom, R., Chesterman, J., Luckett, R. and Woods, B. (1990) *Case Management in Social and Health Care: the Gateshead Community Care Scheme*. Canterbury: PSSRU, University of Kent.

CIPFA (Chartered Institute of Public Finance and Accountancy) (1993) *Accounting for Social Services in Great Britain*. London: CIPFA.

Clode, D. (1993) 'Laptop language.' *Community Care* 27 May 1993 29–31.

Davies, B. and Challis, D. (1986) *Matching Resources to Needs in Community Care*. Aldershot: Gower.

Department of Health, Social Services Inspectorate and Scottish Office, Social Work Services Group (1991a) *Care Management and Assessment: Managers' Guide*. London: HMSO.

Department of Health, Social Services Inspectorate and Scottish Office, Social Work Services Group (1991b) *Care Management and Assessment: Practitioners' Guide*. London: HMSO.

Department of Health (1991c) *Implementing Community Care – Purchaser, Commissioner and Provider Roles*. London: HMSO.

Department of Health (1992) *Committed to Quality: Quality Assurance in Social Services Departments*. London: HMSO.

Griffiths, R. (1988) *Community Care: Agenda for Action*. London: HMSO.

Harvey, C. and Philpot, T. (1993) 'Embracing the future.' *Community Care*, 18 November 1993.

Midwinter, A. (1993) 'Local government reform: Taking stock of the Conservative approach.' *Scottish Affairs 5*, 58–71.

National Health Service and Community Care Act 1990. London: HMSO.

Scottish Office (1991a) *Community Care in Scotland – Assessment and Care Management*. Circular SW11/1991. Edinburgh: The Scottish Office.

Social Services Research Group (1988) 'Performance Measurement in Personal Social Services.' Special Issue of *Research, Policy and Planning 6*, 2.

Social Work Research Centre, University of Stirling (1994) *Community Care in Scotland Discussion Papers*. Stirling: University of Stirling.

Tayside Regional Council (1992a) *Social Work Department Community Care Plan*. Dundee: Tayside Regional Council Social Work Department.

Tayside Regional Council (1992b) *Report on Pilot Studies*. Dundee: Tayside Regional Council Social Work Department. Unpublished.

Tayside Regional Council (1993) *Assessment and Care Management; Practice*. Dundee: Tayside Regional Council Social Work Department.

Wagner, G. (chairman) (1988) *Residential Care: A Positive Choice*. London: HMSO.

Chapter 6

Care Management
Meeting Different Needs

Lorna Cameron and Isobel Freeman

The White Paper *Caring for People* (1989) laid great emphasis on proper assessment of need and good care management, describing them as the cornerstones of high quality community care. There has been considerable debate since its publication on what is understood by care management, the relationship between care management and assessment, the point at which care management is required and the difference between existing care management and best practice. There was, however, a clear view that care management should be defined as any process of managing and coordinating services for the individual user in a way that provided continuity of care and accountability to user and agency. It comprised seven core tasks that would be undertaken for all users to varying degrees and in different ways: publishing information, screening, assessment, care planning, implementation of care plan, monitoring and reviewing.[1]

Stalker, Taylor and Petch (1993) suggest that care management differs from traditional social work in a number of ways. It should be needs-led, and primarily aimed at those with complex needs; there should be a care coordinator; budgets should be delegated; and users and carers should be empowered.

This chapter discusses the ways in which assessment and care management, and in particular the core tasks, were approached in a number of selected projects. It considers the extent to which the approach was influenced by the nature of the client group being served, and whether the aims of care management described above were being achieved.

Background to the study

Before finalising the arrangements for developing assessment and care management within Strathclyde Region, it was felt that much could be learned from looking at examples of existing practice in a systematic way. Local managers were asked to complete inventories of current community care services, identifying those which represented examples of good care management practice.

It was in the main work being done by specialist projects which was highlighted as worthy of further investigation. It was clear that for many of the community care client groups, much of the existing experience of assessing clients' needs and coordinating care lay with specialist projects, including disability resource centres, dementia projects and joint community teams, or with home care teams, rather than within generic area teams.

The three key areas on which the evaluations of the selected projects were to focus were: (1) the effectiveness of targeting and identification of those in greatest need; (2) the implementation of a needs-led approach and coordinated case management for all clients in community care; (3) the cost effectiveness of the organisation of current services and of any developments. The evaluation of the selected projects involved an examination of referral and case information, interviews with staff, clients and carers, and consideration of information about costs where this was available.

From these studies a number of general lessons were learned about the delivery of assessment and care management services, and about the needs of different client groups. This review will consider the lessons under the three headings, and comment on differences emerging in the approaches adopted towards clients with different needs.

The client groups covered by the projects evaluated in Strathclyde were elderly people, people with acute or chronic ill health, people with learning disabilities, people with physical disabilities, people requiring end of life care, people suffering from mental health problems and people with dementia. The projects also provided services for carers. (A list of the projects studied is provided in the Appendix.)

Some of the identified projects focused on the needs of one particular client group. These included the community learning disabilities teams, the dementia projects, the community mental health team and projects for people with physical disabilities. Others theoretically provided services for more than one client group, although in practice many of the clients were elderly people. This applied to the home care projects and the home from hospital projects. It should be recognised that many of the clients had a range of problems, for example many clients with learning disabilities also had physical disabilities, and some may also have had mental health problems. Almost all elderly people receiving a service did so because they had needs resulting from ill health, physical disability or dementia. The Social Service Inspectorate Report (Department of Health 1993) on assessment and care management stated that they did not find significant differences in the way assessment and care management were being applied to older people and people with a physical disability, but did not discuss other client groups.

Clients defined within a particular client group may therefore have had different needs from one another, and may have had needs similar to clients in another client group. Such classifications of need are useful only when their limitations are recognised. As the organisation of most social work departments and services is based on client groups, exploring the extent to which approaches differ depending on the client groups will help assess the value of such a form of organisation.

Targeting and publicity

The key tasks central to targeting and identifying those in greatest need are publishing information and screening clients. At the time the projects were set up there was very little publicity material produced by the Department which described the assistance available to clients requiring to be supported in the community and to have packages of care coordinated.

On the whole the selected projects provided good publicity materials. A few projects, however, had difficulty preparing appropriate publicity material, and initially some projects were worried that they might create too great a demand prior to being properly established. This was particularly true for projects providing a service for clients with few services available to them. For example, one project seeking to develop self advocacy services for clients with disabilities found itself receiving large numbers of referrals from clients seeking general information about services; and one of the projects offering support to clients suffering from severe dementia found it also received a large number of requests for advice and assistance from clients with a mild form of confusion. It was felt that some leaflets should be addressed to client groups explaining not only what community care services in general were available, but also what services were available to meet some of the particular needs of the client group.

The evaluation of the projects highlighted the need for clear eligibility criteria. The Social Services Inspectorate Report (Department of Health 1993) criticised the authorities they reviewed for not making eligibility criteria universally available. In the projects we examined, even when the criteria for referral were clearly laid out, there were inappropriate referrals. There was a need to ensure that inappropriate referrals were referred on to an appropriate unit that would provide an assessment or service, or that if no appropriate unit was available, that information about this area of unmet need was fed into the planning system.

Several of the projects found there was very little information on services and resources for particular client groups, and tried to build up resource directories and information banks. (The Social Services Inspectorate Report had also found that staff experienced difficulty in obtaining information to facilitate user choice and develop imaginative responses to need.) Information was particularly difficult to obtain on resources for clients with head injuries, and with chronic physical illnesses and disabilities. There was also very little information available on services other than training centre provision for clients with learning disabilities. This was partly because of a lack of resources for these client groups, but also because existing resources were some distance away and therefore were not known locally. Another problem was the fact that clients may have had additional needs or particular needs which meant that only some facilities were suitable. For example, one client with a physical disability who required respite facilities found no registered residential or nursing home in Scotland able or willing to deal with her particular disability. If clients are to be empowered, the provision of good resource information is essential, especially in the field of physical disability but also for all client groups.

Implementation of a needs-led approach and care management

Assessment and care planning

It is important to stress that assessment was not a single event, but an ongoing process which was often time consuming, and it was the process which was evaluated. The selected projects were expected to deal with complex assessments. No clear definition of what should constitute a complex case was provided, although it was suggested that clients generally would require more than one service. The complexity of cases varied greatly. It was found that for some clients with particular needs the process was lengthy, for example Case Study 1.

Case Study 1

The client who was 66 years old, was paralysed, and was in the spinal unit of a local hospital at the time she was referred to the project by the Community Occupational Therapist. An initial assessment was carried out while the client was in hospital, and a further assessment was conducted in the client's home by the occupational therapist. Additional information was provided by the hospital and the Housing Department.

The needs identified included helping the client in and out of bed; assistance to turn in bed; and help to bath the client. The resources identified included housing adaptations, home support, a hoist, a bed, and a wheelchair. Discussions were held with the project staff about the immediate needs of the client, and to organise an initial care plan. A case conference was convened by the hospital consultant. Some difficulties were experienced at the conference: the nursing staff were unable to commit resources, and the client and carers found it difficult to participate fully in the proceedings.

A month later, another case conference was held at the request of the project leader. The consultant felt that the client could be nursed at home until her skin had healed, after which she could return to hospital for rehabilitation. The client was unable to finance home care and was not eligible for Independent Living Fund money. The project leader was unable to arrange transferring funding from the health board in order to pay for the client's care.

When the client was visited in hospital she expressed concern about returning home before her skin had finally healed. After four months, the client was still in hospital and the case was on-going.

For other clients it was more straightforward, as in Case Study 2.

Case Study 2

The client was aged 72, and had recently been discharged from hospital following major surgery. Nursing care was organised to enable her to recuperate in her own home. The client's wound did not heal properly, and therefore she needed an intensive range of services for the first four months, until she was able to do things for herself.

The Home Help Organiser visited the client after she was discharged from hospital to discuss her needs. A full assessment of the client's needs was arranged, although with some difficulty as the client had preconceived ideas about the Social Work department, and felt that the assessment process was a very long and involved one in order just to receive a home help. The client was assessed as needing help with household tasks, with meals, and as requiring an occupational therapy assessment. Although the client was offered meals on wheels, as well as a home help, she refused, preferring to have only a home help.

The Home Help Organiser felt that the assessment had been appropriate and sufficiently thorough, although she would have preferred the occupational therapist assessment to have been organised sooner. The Home Help Organiser attempted, as far as was possible, to conduct a needs-led assessment, although this was difficult as the client kept focusing on services.

The views of both the client and carer were considered. Initially, the client was in a very poor state, so the carer arranged services with the Home Help Organiser.

The client felt that her views were taken into account, although she said that she relied on staff to tell her what services were available. She received a home help service to help with washing, dressing, meals, shopping, and general tasks as required. The client said that she could not have managed without the service.

All staff stressed the importance of adopting a needs-led approach to assessment but recognised that it took time to develop such an approach. Many staff within social work and in other agencies found the transition to a needs led philosophy difficult. In addition, clients who were used to requesting specific services found it difficult to identify their needs. The

Social Services Inspectorate Report suggested that there was a tradition of the public and other agencies expecting services to be provided following minimal investigation.

The projects dealing with elderly people were, in the main, home care projects and were developments of existing provision, giving the home care organiser the ability to arrange further services for other client groups. The projects were providing clients with an opportunity to discuss their needs, and to help prepare a care package. Many of the clients with physical and learning disabilities had been in receipt of services in the past, but had received no comprehensive assessment. The projects provided them with a full assessment and care package.

Staff acknowledged the importance of taking the client's views and the views of their carers into account. Difficulties arose however, when different members of a family had conflicting needs. These difficulties were also highlighted by Stalker *et al.* (1993). Most projects agreed that generally it was the client's needs and views which were given priority. The following two case studies provide examples of this.

Case Study 3

The client was aged 18, and had cerebral palsy. He was severely mentally and physically disabled. The client lived with his mother (his father lived in the house part time). The parents had a second child who also had a severe learning disability, and was in residential care. The family had been known to the social work department for a number of years, and various social workers had been involved with them, including the key assessor.

The assessment process was judged to have been sufficiently thorough, and involved the appropriate agencies, although it was felt that at times it could have been more intensive. The key assessor consulted reports prepared by other teams, including the community team, and all the relevant people were brought together during a review meeting.

The assessor felt that the client needed a warm and loving home environment which, it seemed, he had never experienced. She felt that the carer, who was often drinking while caring for her son, had dictated her own position to the social work department for some time, and that this had been allowed to happen at the client's expense. His case, but not his needs, had been known and unresolved for years. Staff felt that had the client been a child care case, he would previously have been taken into residential care, and they were looking into the legal implications of a guardianship order, to decide whether or not it would be possible to pursue this course.

A range of options was considered, including expanding the flexicare services, already provided, and the possibility of shared care. In addition, the carer was being offered home help services, which, along with flexi-care would enable the family situation to be regularly monitored. The case was on-going, and the final decision about services had still to be taken.

Case Study 4

This client, who was aged 36 and had a learning disability, lived with her brother who had moved into the family home after the death of their father, and signed a shared tenancy on behalf of the client in order to live there. The social worker, who had been involved with the client for a number of years, was concerned that she was being abused by her brother, who appeared to harass and upset her.

The client was a very sociable person who had been emotionally and environmentally deprived. When upset, the client became uncontrolled and a danger to herself and those around her. Recently she had been given a lot of individual attention, including personal care and help with her finances, to which she responded well. The client wanted to have her own flat and to continue with her day placement at the centre.

The client had to move to a local hostel because of harassment from her brother and, as a consequence, efforts were made to either remove her brother from the house so that the client could live there with appropriate support, or persuade the District Council to allocate another house to her. The immediate plan was that the client would be kept away from the family home until the situation with her brother was resolved. She was due to go on holiday, after which she was to have a period of sheltered care.

After a court hearing the client's brother was admitted to a psychiatric unit, during which time the client managed to live on her own with home help support. Her brother continued to claim that she was incapable of living on her own.

The danger of colluding with carers, especially when clients had communication difficulties, was highlighted by a number of workers. Many
carers, particularly carers of adults with learning disabilities, found the
emphasis on the client's views to be a major shift in the approach of the
social work department.

Case Study 5

This client was aged 18 and was emotionally unstable and very
insecure. She had recently finished a very difficult school career and
her father refused to care for her unless he received the assistance he
wanted.

The client's behaviour deteriorated, and she was not responding well
to the two social workers she knew well. Staff at the centre she
attended felt that it was not the most suitable environment to meet
the client's needs. Her mother, however, was planning to take action
against the social work department for failing to provide her daughter with services to meet her needs. Staff, however, did not feel that
a busy environment was a suitable placement for a person not able
to interact well with people.

Time requires to be spent with carers to explain the social work department's philosophy, especially with the change in approach and greater
focus on empowering clients. This is particularly important in the case of
clients with learning disabilities and young physically disabled people.

In the case of some of the disability and home from hospital projects,
following the wishes of clients sometimes resulted in carers feeling that
an immense burden had been placed on them. This was partly due to their
previous experiences of receiving limited support.

In some projects the assessment was kept separate from service provision while in others some or all services were directly provided by the
assessor. The separation of service provision from the assessment was
found to cause problems in some cases when staff had to rely on someone
else to provide the service, as it was harder to coordinate the package. On
the other hand, when dealing with the complex needs of many of the
clients with physical and learning disabilities, staff found it very difficult
to act as assessor and provider. Home care staff who were required both
to carry out assessments and to provide services in cases with a lesser

degree of complexity did not find these roles conflicting. Some, however, found it difficult to manage both aspects of their work.

The focused approach adopted by many of the projects, resulting from their clear aims and objectives and strict eligibility criteria, resulted in their successfully planning and managing care packages with and for clients. Area teams had at that time limited experience of the care planning work being undertaken by community teams, dementia projects and disability resource centres. Many of the clients receiving support from the community teams and disability projects had previously been involved with social work area teams, but the assistance provided had generally been short term and was described by some clients as impersonal and unfocused. A number of projects worked with clients who had been known to the social work department for some time but whose need for care had not previously been comprehensively assessed and who had not received coordinated packages of care. Clients appreciated adaptable services and seemed less confused by the delivery of services when one person was coordinating their care package.

Case Study 6

The carers (a sister and brother-in-law) of one of the clients interviewed were asked for their views. The carers were able to compare the community team input to previous social work involvement, and felt that previous services had lacked coordination and continuity. In addition, the carers felt that in the past the onus had been on the client or carer to contact services they felt they required. There had also been several changes of social workers, and at one stage the client's case was closed, and then re-opened.

The carers liked the fact that the community team offered a specialised service for people with learning disabilities, and the fact that it enabled a number of professionals to work together as a team. Over the previou
s eight months there had been several meetings arranged which included all the professional staff involved in their brother's care. The carers felt that this was excellent as it provided an opportunity for those involved to discuss problem areas and possible solutions. The main areas of intervention included appropriate use of money, dietary issues, use of leisure time, and medication, house decoration and repairs. The carers felt that over the period there had been some

improvement in all of the above areas, whereas very little had been done to address these issues in the past.

All the projects evaluated tried to offer choices to clients. It has to be acknowledged that these choices were often limited by a lack of resources, and that the extent of this problem varied from project to project depending on the area in which it was located, and the client group served. Some areas, for example, had limited respite, home support and day care resources available, and there were few resources available for people with a head injury. There was also a need for more imaginative services for people with physical disabilities. Despite the limitations, clients did appreciate being given a choice, but there was a need to develop understanding of empowerment and self advocacy.

Case Study 7

The client was referred by his son after their home help had given them a leaflet about the project. The client was receiving home help services twice a week, but his son was concerned about a deterioration in his well-being, and the fact that he seemed to be depressed and lonely, and not managing at home. The client's son said that he had temporarily to give up his business in order to care for his father.

The services were provided in line with the assessment. The home help input was increased from two to seven days a week, and the client attended a lunch club. In addition, he had several rooms redecorated, and was waiting to have some aids put in to his house. The client was given options, and decided not to attend a day centre or to accept an alarm system. Although these alternative packages were costed, cost did not influence the final decision, whereas client choice did.

Projects generally met the needs they identified as far as resources allowed. Sometimes where needs identified were not met it was because clients did not want the services offered, preferring to cope on their own as much as they could. This was true of all client groups. Some projects explicitly recognised the importance of ensuring they did not foster over-dependence, while others were less aware of the importance of this philosophy. Staff who did discuss it were very aware of the difficulties in achieving a balance between minimum intervention and enabling the client and his or her family to achieve a reasonable quality of life. This was especially problematic when clients and their families expected so little in the way of support, and often had difficulty in identifying their needs.

Monitoring and reviewing

Most, although not all, of the projects provided written plans. About half of the projects evaluated gave the written plans to clients. Clients seemed to like being given care plans, especially those presented in the format of a timetable as they found them easier to understand. In projects which dealt with clients whose needs were continually changing, keeping written plans up to date proved to be time-consuming and difficult. This was particularly true of clients suffering from acute or chronic illnesses, and elderly clients. Despite this, staff recognised the completion of plans as necessary in order that to monitor the use of resources and highlight unmet need.

Staff had review meetings with all clients. Reviews were held at agreed intervals and were relatively formal. Meetings varied in size, ranging from relatively small meetings involving the client and the key worker, to large scale meetings involving all interested parties and agencies. Some clients were uncomfortable about the formality of reviews and found them quite stressful. Generally, clients appeared to prefer reviews to involve as few people as possible, although there were some clients who appreciated on occasions having all agencies involved in their case together at the one time. This was true of all client groups.

The frequency of reviews varied greatly depending on the project, the client group served and the individual cases. In some of the home from hospital projects, reviews took place a week after the service was provided because there was a need for the early planning of the withdrawal of service. In other projects quarterly reviews were seen as more appropriate, and in others annual reviews. For those with relatively stable conditions, for example people with learning disabilities and some types of physical disabilities, annual reviews were adequate. For clients whose condition was fluctuating or deteriorating reviews were required much more often.

Clients involved with different parts of social work services and other agencies were often confused about the respective roles of staff. This confusion was at times exacerbated by a lack of coordination of services. For example, some clients with learning disabilities were reviewed by their community team social worker and soon after a review at their adult training centre. There was clearly a need to coordinate the review process and ensure that an appropriate person was identified as care coordinator.

For clients with learning disabilities this could be a social worker, or their day care key worker. For elderly clients the home care organiser often acted as care manager, although in some cases a social worker or social work assistant was seen as more appropriate. Strathclyde was only one of two Regions in Scotland where home care organisers acted as care managers (Stalker *et al.* 1993).

Costs and budgetary control

Most projects had devolved management, although control over budgets and use of resources had not necessarily been devolved. Projects which had greater control over resources generally found it easier to make flexible care arrangements. Where the use of the budget was limited to specific services, staff felt restricted and preferred complete devolution of budgetary control. It was more likely to be home care projects which had devolved budgets. Projects dealing with very complex cases, involving relatively costly care plans, did not generally have devolved budgets.

Packages of care tended not to be formally costed. Generally, client choice and the availability of resources influenced their inclusion in a care package. Staff rarely had a wide range of options to choose from, especially in the case of clients with physical and learning disabilities, and were seldom in a position to be able to opt for a certain package because it cost less.

Calculating costs when comparing admission to hospital or residential care with the cost of community support was relatively easy. There were very few examples of residential care being chosen because it was cheaper, although there were examples of moves from hospital to the community being delayed because money for home care was not available. It was more difficult to assess the impact of cost considerations when residential or hospital care was not the immediate alternative, and when it was a question of how much support was necessary to keep the client from further deteriorating, and what level of quality of life should be aimed for.

The cost of assessments and reviews was an issue, and in the individual reports on projects an attempt has been made to detail the cost of an assessment and a review. The cost is illustrated by the following example.

Cost of assessment

The project was only available to people with very complex needs who required a care coordinator. As a result, it was very time consuming and costly. From the information received on the assessments, the average assessment took ten hours, and cost approximately £86.00. Added to this, the cost of one and a half hours' administration (£7.65), one hour of phone calls (£3.60), and an average of 28 miles travelled (at 33p per mile, £9.24) brought the average total cost to £106.49. Simpler assessments were much less expensive.

In most cases, but not all, the level of assessment of clients which was undertaken, and the frequency of reviews, was in line with their level of need. In some cases, however, staff felt that the level of assessment of some clients was too detailed. Occasionally it was felt that the review of cases could have been undertaken less frequently than originally planned. One of the community teams originally planned to review cases every three months, but found annual reviews to be sufficient.

The concern of staff to meet the needs of clients, encouraged by the training courses run for project staff, led to a greater flexibility in the way staff approached their work. Home help staff were happy to undertake a much wider range of tasks than was traditionally the case. Volunteers were also used in a variety of projects. This, in some cases, helped keep costs down. Projects differed in their views about whether they felt the use of part-time or sessional staff was appropriate. Using sessional staff allowed more flexibility and was more cost effective. However, it caused problems when dealing with particular client groups, such as people with dementia, as staff involved frequently moved on to permanent employment, resulting in new staff having to be trained, and the loss of continuity with clients and carers. For many clients the key times that help was required was in the evenings, during the night and at weekends. This could prove to be expensive, depending on the conditions of service under which staff were employed. It was in that area that most conflict around costs arose.

Conclusion

The assessment and care management process was essentially the same for all client groups, but for some, aspects of the process were more difficult than for others.

The development of assessment and care management services resulted in home care organisers being able to coordinate a wider range of services for elderly clients and clients in acute hospitals. For clients with learning disabilities and physical disabilities the development was even more radical with clients receiving full assessments and coordinated care packages for the first time. For such clients, the assessment process was lengthy, and the care packages provided could be expensive.

For clients with physical disabilities and chronic physical illnesses and, to a lesser extent, dementia, there was a lack of resources generally available, and a lack of information about the resources which did exist. For clients with physical disabilities and learning disabilities the range of resources available was also limited, with many projects stating that there was a need for more innovative services to be developed. As a result of this lack of information and resources for these client groups, projects could not fully empower clients and offer them a choice of services.

A great deal of care was taken to ensure that the views of clients and carers were taken into account. In all client groups this could create problems when the views of the carers and clients were divergent and in many of the cases difficult family relationships were a feature. For carers of clients with learning disabilities, the focus on empowering clients was a change in approach and many found this difficult to come to terms with. This was also a problem for some carers of elderly clients and clients with physical disabilities who were used to making decisions on behalf of the person they cared for. In some cases empowering clients and developing their ability to live independently did place additional burdens on carers.

Although the needs of some clients were relatively stable, the needs of many clients, particularly clients with physical illness, dementia and mental health problems, changed frequently. For such clients, there was a need to constantly monitor, and regularly review their needs, reducing as well as increasing services as required.

Projects which had experience of managing devolved budgets found this a positive experience, although some projects took some time to make use of their budgets. The sums of money involved were not large and there was a need further to develop the use of devolved budgets.

In conclusion, in line with the spirit of the community care legislation, the client's needs and wishes appeared to be much greater influences than cost considerations on the services provided in the vast majority of individual cases. However, there is no doubt that lack of resources is inhibiting the development of innovative community support projects and this limits choice for clients.

Appendix

List of projects evaluated, by client groups covered

Group 1: Disability or Centre Based Project

Monklands Disability Resource Centre	Physically disabled people
North East Project	Physically disabled people
Robert Owen Centre	People with physical and learning disabilities

Group 2: Community Teams

North West Community Mental Handicap Team	People with learning disabilities
Monklands Community Learning Disabilities Team	People with learning disabilities
Monklands Community Mental Health Team	People with mental health problems
Clydebank Area Team	Elderly people

Group 3: Home Care Projects

Paisley Home Care	All community care client, groups, but mainly elderly
South West Home Care/Hospice Project	End of life care
North West Home Care	All community care client groups, but mainly elderly
South Ayr Home Care	All community care client groups, but mainly elderly

Group 4: Home From Hospital Projects

Ayrshire Central Project	All community care client groups
Southern General Project	All community care client groups
Lightburn Project	All community care client groups
Inverclyde	All community care client groups

Group 5: Dementia Projects

Inverclyde Dementia Care Project	People with dementia
South Ayr Dementia Project	People with dementia

References

Caring for People: Community Care in the Next Decade and Beyond (1989). Cm 849. London: HMSO.

Stalker, K., Taylor. J., and Petch. A. (1994) *Implementing Community Care in Scotland: Early Snapshots*. Community Care in Scotland Discussion Paper No 4. Stirling: Social Work Research Centre, University of Stirling.

Department of Health, Social Services Inspectorate (1993) *Inspection of Assessment and Care Management Arrangements in Social Services Departments: Interim Overview Report*. London: HMSO.

Chapter 7

Costs, Budgets and Community Care

Irvine Lapsley

This chapter addresses the issues surrounding costs and budgets in community care in two ways: (1) by examining the origins and pressures for a greater visibility for accounting measures such as costings and budgets in social care and (2) by considering available evidence on the actual and potential consequences of this accounting agenda in social care. In the discussion of (1), consideration is not only given to tracing the origins of the trend towards greater weight being attached to accounting techniques (such as costs and budgets), but also to the tensions around the 'accounting model'. The second part of this chapter considers both the consequences of an increased emphasis on costs and budgets in terms of the *modus operandi* of social services, and also its likely impacts on the values embedded in the social care area. The picture presented is one of complexity – both on the part of the origins and alleged benefits of costings and devolved budgets and also in the implications of implementing these accounting technologies in social services.

Costs and budgets: a new visibility

The emphasis on costing information and the pressure for devolved budgets can be seen as necessary components of the new arrangements for community care, in which a quasi-market is promoted with care managers at the centre (as purchasers) making decisions on meeting the social care needs of individuals, but with due regard to the cost implications of specific choices and the overall impact of such decisions on the resources at their disposal. This is (part) of the theory of the new quasi-market in social care, and the extent to which the above description of what was intended corresponds with what happens, in practice, is considered in the following section. However, it is important to note that this new visibility for accounting measures and models is part of a much larger phenomenon within the public services – the 'new managerialism'. Recognition of this phenomenon should carry with it a critical assessment of the transportability or portability of private sector accounting practices for public service organisations. Hood (1991) has identified the key components of this (to use his term) 'New Public Management' as comprising the following:

1. *Hands-on professional management in the public sector*

    This entails the identification of named individuals at the top of the organisation with accountability through clear assignment of responsibility for action.

2. *Explicit standards and measures of performance*

    This involves the use of quantitative measures of goals and objectives and of their attainment (or otherwise).

3. *Greater emphasis on output controls*

    This shifts the focus to results rather than procedures, with explicit links between rewards and performance.

4. *The shift to disaggregation of units in the public sector*

    In the pursuit of 'efficiency', more manageable units of provision, with devolved budgets, replace large scale public sector organisations.

5. *Shift to greater competition in the public sector*

    This is evident in the use of compulsory competitive tendering and other market pressures to reduce costs.

6. *Stress on private sector styles of management practice*

    The abandonment of the public service ethos and its replacement by more aggressive private sector management which use techniques such as accounting in their rewards/performance control structures.

7. *Stress on greater discipline and parsimony in resource use*

    Cost reduction and value for money – 'the need to do more with less'.

In all of these components, accounting has a role to play. There is the explicit role as a technique of private sector management (see 6 above), but also as a means of quantifying performance (2 and 3 above), assisting in the identification of least costly alternatives (5 and 7 above) and as the central tool by which the pursuit of efficiency is achieved – the use of devolved budgets (4 above). It can be seen, therefore, that while the prime component of individual managerial responsibility and accountability (see 1 above) is the driving force for this dramatic change in service delivery, accounting is a vehicle for making this process work. In particular, in the central area of devolved budgets and cost management, the ideas of the new managerialism sweeping through the public sector find expression. However, this 'accounting model' carries with it its own tensions and difficulties and the over-zealous adoption, without effective adaptation, by public service organisations may pose problems and have dysfunctional consequences for service delivery. Some of these issues are addressed, next.

The classic difficulties around the notion of the devolved budget are those in which this is not perceived by those involved in its implementation as a technical, neutral guide to action but as a game. There is now a voluminous literature on gaming behaviour in budgets, which cannot be fully covered within this chapter. However, a useful starting point is to note the opportunities for gaming behaviour, which negate the vision of the new public sector management as dealing in 'facts'. There are thirty such ploys identified by Anthony and Herzlinger (1994, pp.500–508). These are grouped according to whether (1) there is a new programme or activity, (2) there is a need to maintain or increase existing programmes, (3) cuts in expenditure may be imposed and (4) ploys engaged by managers (see Table 7.1). Many of these ploys are evident from the description accorded them, others are not so and a few are briefly explained here. For example, ploy 2, the 'hidden ball', means the (concealed) inclusion of a politically unattractive programme by hiding it within an attractive programme; ploy 5, the 'shell game', is the use of statistics to give a misleading picture of the true state of affairs; ploy 19, 'sprinkling', is the increase in budget estimates by a few per cent, often in areas difficult to detect, in anticipation of arbitrary, across-the-board cuts in expenditure; ploy 21, 'Gold Watch', is a response which will do more harm than good to requests for cuts in expenditure (this is based on a manager's proposal to eliminate gold watches to retiring employees, instead of attempting to make other cuts); ploy 25, 'End Run', is going outside normal channels to obtain the

Table 7.1: Budget Ploys

Ploys for New Programmes

1.   Foot in the Door
2.   Hidden Ball
3.   Divide and Conquer
4.   Distraction
5.   Shell Game
6.   It's free
7.   Implied Top-level Support
8.   You're to Blame
9.   Nothings Too good for Our People
10. Keeping up with the Joneses
11. We Must be Up-to-date
12. If We Don't Someone Else Will
13. Call it a Rose
14. Outside Experts

Ploys for Maintaining or Increasing Existing Programmes

15. Show of Strength
16. Razzle-Dazzle
17. Delayed Buck
18. Reverence for the Past
19. Sprinkling

Ploys to Resist Cuts

20. Make a Study
21. Gold Watch
22. Arouse Client Antagonism
23. Witches and Goblins
24. We are the Experts
25. End Run

Ploys Primarily for Managers

26. Keep Them Lean and Hungry
27. Productivity Cuts
28. Arbitrary Cuts
29. Only Work Here
30. Make a Study

Source: adapted from Anthony and Young, Management Control in Non Profit Organisations, fifth edition, R.D.Irwin, 1994, pp.500–508.

reversal of a decision to make expenditure cuts. These ploys may be employed, within organisations (which raises doubts about the adoption of such techniques as ensuring 'efficiency') or between public sector organisations and some higher authority or funding body (which casts doubts on this mechanism as a device for ensuring accountability of such organisations).

This suggests that proponents of the 'new managerialism' in public services will be satisfied that the *presence* of budgets in public sector organisations will give the impression (accurate or otherwise) of a rational, efficiently-run operation, which means that their *existence* is synonymous with 'good management'. But there have been attacks on the nature of budgets as devices for assisting the management of organisations, as the critique by Mintzberg (1975) of (private sector) budgets and information systems demonstrates. In this critique, Mintzberg stresses the needs of management for information in conditions of high environmental uncertainty (i.e. information about unfamiliar events) whereas budgets focus on easy-to-measure, routine events. Other characteristics of such formal information systems are (1) the emphasis on events internal to the organisation to the exclusion of events in the external environment (2) an inability to capture the complexity and unpredictability of changes in the environment (3) a focus on historical information which is inadequate in an environment of rapid, unpredictable change.[1] All of this points to the necessity to examine closely the premises and practices of such management control techniques before transplanting them to the public sector situation, the more so because of the particular complexities of the public sector (of outcome measurement, political pressure undermining financial discipline, inadequate knowledge of means-end relationships which makes procedures more rather than less important). As Brunsson (1994) puts it, in many public sector organisations, overspending on the budget can be portrayed as success, rather than failure, in terms of service delivery. It also mobilises arguments for the resourcing of current needs and, in this way, the budget as a device around which resource allocation decisions are made serves numerous, subtle purposes which presents a

---

1   It should be noted that, at the time of writing, and subsequently, Mintzberg's criticisms of accounting practices held true. However, in the past decade, there has been a shift in focus to *strategic management accounting* which addresses at least some of Mintzberg' concerns (particularly by the inclusion of external events such as benchmarking) but there is little evidence of such techniques being widely applied in either the private or public sectors.

challenge for the unthinking application of private sector techniques, such as accounting, to public sector settings. The outcome of the adoption of costs and devolved budgets within the social services is examined below against the above background of pressures (questionable, legitimate, or otherwise) for a greater visibility for accounting in social services in the new community care era.

Costs and budgets in social care – actual and potential consequences

As mentioned above, the concept of the budget is not new to public sector organisations, such as local authorities. Indeed, for many years the budget has been the cornerstone of financial planning for such organisations, particularly in local government. However, the current move to the quasi-market has changed the manner of budgeting in two significant ways: (1) the intended devolution of budgets to care managers at lower levels of responsibility than previously and (2) this, in tandem with a switch from overall control of outturns on an aggregate basis (committee by committee and for the local authority, in total) to the use of costs for specific services and activities. Both of these dimensions create a new visibility for accounting numbers and leave open the possibility that financial discipline assumes a primacy over, or at least equates to, the traditional values of social service staff (of client choice, confidentiality, dignity and so on). The actual and potential consequences of this new thrust are explored below in two, quite different ways. First, the results of a survey (Stalker, Taylor and Petch 1994) are examined. This gives a picture of practical responses to the need for devolved budgets in Scottish local authorities. Second, the results of a study of decision-makers within the new contract-setting regime in Scottish local authorities casts light on the significance attached to the costing dimension in social care, and the extent to which values embedded within social care are attenuated by this new visibility for accounting (Lapsley and Llewellyn 1994). Each of these studies is considered below, in turn.

The Stalker *et al.* (1994) survey revealed a diversity of practices in terms of the *level* at which budgets were held within Scottish local authorities (see Table 7.2). The general picture is one of limited devolution of budgets with some declarations of intent to devolve further, notably in the case of the Western Isles which aims to do so to care manager level. Major constraints on such developments noted by Stalker *et al.* were (1) the difficulty of switching budgets which traditionally had a service focus (e.g. residential, daycare or domiciliary services) rather than on the needs of individuals and (2) an absence of computerised financial information

Table 7.2: Level of budget holder responsibility

Regional Authority	Budget Holder
Borders	Divisional Operations Managers
Tayside	Cost Centre Managers
Shetland	Divisional Managers
Grampian	Divisional Managers
Dumfries & Galloway	Operational Principal Social Workers District Managers
Lothian	District Managers
Strathclyde	Regional Managers
Fife	Community Care Senior*
Orkney	Area Team Managers*
Highland	Team Managers*
Central	Team Managers*
Western Isles	Care Managers*

* planned
Source: Stalker, Taylor and Petch (1994).

systems which were both user friendly and had the capability of generating complex financial and statistical information. This study observed some modest steps in this direction by the practice of giving small (a figure of £30,000 is cited by Stalker *et al.*, in relation to home-based support in one regional authority) sums to individual teams. This was described in one region as 'giving permission to be imaginative at a local level' (Stalker *et al.*, p.26). Overall, this study concluded that the approach of local authorities in Scotland towards devolved budgets was 'cautious'.

A similar story was found in relation to the second dimension of accounting visibility, that is, the costs of specific services or activities. In this study, the authors summarise the position of the Scottish local authorities, as follows (Stalker *et al.* 1994).

> 'Lothian and Highland were working on the basis of notional costs, whilst calculating "real" equivalents. Western Isles had "rough" costings so far, but were considering making each user a cost centre. Other regions, for example, Fife, Dumfries and Galloway and Orkney had completed costings for specific services including residential care and domiciliary care. Strathclyde were grappling with a different set of problems. Costs for specific services vary throughout the region; consequently, they were trying to develop a method of standardisation. Borders were at the stage of evolving methodologies, whereas Shetland had not yet commenced the process and "won't for some time". The two regions furthest down the road were Grampian and Central. The former has completed its costings and the latter stated that work on this area was almost accomplished.' (p.87)

The above picture – of services which have incomplete devolution of budgets and for which unit costing information is not generally available – suggests that the new financial discipline will have had limited impact on the minds and actions of social workers grappling with the purchaser/provider split, the need for contracting and the expectation that a more 'entrepreneurial' spirit will be exhibited by social workers at the nexus of decisions on social care and resource utilisation. Some indication of the extent of, and meaning of, this spread of costs and budgetary information through social work departments is obtained from the second study (Lapsley and Llewellyn 1994). The nature of this investigation and some key findings are set out below.

This second study builds upon previous research into the costs and quality of care provided in the mixed economy of residential care for the elderly (Bland *et al.* 1992). Within this study by Lapsley and Llewellyn (1994), the major focus was on the decision-makers responsible for contract-setting in the new community care regime. The project proceeded by presenting two sets of data (1) a simple dataset of costs and quality of care scores and (2) a more complex dataset, comprising the constituent elements of both the costs and quality of care scores, with a set of case studies of possible referrals to residential care, to those responsible for contract-setting in social work departments in the Scottish regions. This usually comprised a contracts officer (although different names for this function were in evidence), a senior social worker and a finance officer. Initial contacts revealed the different patterns of dealing with community care which were emerging in the Scottish regional authorities, as evidenced by the different approaches to contracting. Key findings of this study are examined below by focusing on two strands: (1) the use of cost information and (2) the nature of devolved budgets.

As regards the first of these, the *use of cost information*, this revealed the complexity of the value-driven, rules-based procedures for dealing with problems of social care with which costing information did not readily relate. This is a different order of difficulty from that reported upon by Stalker *et al*. Here the difficulty is not just the derivation of unit cost information by local authority finance departments, but the complexity of the decision processes which makes connections with costing information problematic. There was also evidence of the difficulties experienced by finance departments in shifting from the budget as a focus of control to the need for costs for activities and services. Here, our information corroborated that of Stalker *et al*., in that cost information was not filtering down to key decision-makers. In this study, when confronted with *costs and quality* of care information there was a tendency to rely on other reference points than the costings, notably 'codes of professional conduct' – in particular, the 'voice' of the client.

However, when presented with the simulated information, there was an interest taken in specific types of costs by these decision-makers, notably, (1) wages costs and (2) capital charges. This, in turn, also reflected professional codes of conduct over what constituted 'value'. In general, high wages were equated with high quality, and vice-versa. This suggests an attenuation of the purchaser/provider split in which purchasers still act as if they are part of an integrated organisation with an almost 'custodial relationship' or concern with 'fair play' arguments over the level of wages of provider organisations. Also, on capital charges there was some concern expressed over the position of private sector operators who could have been in difficulties, but little or no concern about the higher capital costs of local authorities (which are calculated on a different basis) which were taken for granted.

In practice, however, the issue of unit costing information had become a matter of limited importance in the decision-making of those local authority officers. By the use of systems of fixed price contracting, in which the reference point of the level of DSS support (as computed by government for those entitled to 'preserved rights', because they were placed in a residential facility before 1 April 1993) was used as the basic price, there was little or no need to address the provider costs.[2] This had the attraction of reducing uncertainty for social work departments coming to grips with markets in social care. It also sidesteps the problem alluded to above of noise in cost comparisons across sectors of provision (local authority, private, voluntary) because of differences in accounting measurement. It could be argued that this is also indirect evidence of a loose specification in contract setting, if the argument is accepted that tighter contracts would place greater reliance on, and specify the structure of, provider costs. It could also be argued that this focus on fixed prices ignores provider costs, whether expressed in terms of the efficiency of provider units, or the wider issues of responsibility for the continuity of this provision of social care, such that it is not threatened by financial insecurity or failure. This then, is a story of the limited impact of costing information, not simply because of the availability issue of what finance departments can generate, but also of resistance from embedded values, failure to connect with social work decision processes, and an unfolding market which evolves in a manner (fixed price contracts) which undermines a predicted reliance on unit costing information.

On (2) the nature of devolved budgets, this study, by using an indirect and contrasting approach to Stalker *et al.*, provides evidence which corroborates that study's findings, but also adds to our understanding of devolved budgets by examining 'devolved budgets in practice' from a more contextual perspective. In the first instance, the findings of this study suggest that, while devolved budget implementation is going through a transitional phase, there is evidence both that (1) devolved budgets are apparent, but uneven in their filtering down the organisation and (2) the codes and values of social workers remain important in determining courses of action. For example, in relation to (2) above, there tend to be references to other mechanisms (such as registration of, and inspection of, homes for the elderly) which simplify the contract-setting process and result in 'soft' contracts.

These limitations on the impact of devolved budgets are also accentuated by a number of other factors – both at a macro and micro-processual

---

2   This state of affairs cannot exist indefinitely. It provides a means by which social work departments can operate without reference to costs, in the short run. Over the longer term, as the proportion of the population with 'protected' status diminishes, this option will no longer be available to social work departments.

level – which undermine the idea of the devolved budget as a (financial) boundary which constrains activities within the organisation. Thus, at one level, there are well recognised difficulties of overlap and grey areas between health board and local authority budgets. Also, *within* local authorities there are instances of 'member thresholds', in which a commitment is made to underwrite social services by the local authority, which is likely to negate the effects of lower level budgets. Similar difficulties *within* local authorities include (1) the shifting, competing nature of budgets which may result, for example, in a local authority provider being regarded as a 'free good' (2) the fragmentation of budgets (Stalker *et al.* cite some examples of this, also) which may appear to provide 'innovation' but is more likely to lead to sub-optimal behaviour and (3) the failure of these devolved budgets to reach the 'responsive level' of activity (initially thought to be care manager level in these reforms). Finally, the devolved budgets have implicit boundaries for individual managers which determine incentives and penalties. These can also be seen as ill-fitting tó the task. Thus the basic model implicit in the devolved budget is that of 'participation to achieve effectiveness' which is a simple behavioural model, even if there are variants, for example the allowing of discretion or the use of financial incentives. But care managers who do not accept the values implicit in this model may be faced by the costs (loss of resource) of continual efficiency pressures without rewards to which they relate. On the other side of the coin, the use of penalties may prove to be ambiguous because of the difficulty of demonstrating cause and effect. This may lead to fudging or the carry forward of deficits – a mechanism which weakens financial discipline, if the budget holder never catches up.

Conclusion

This chapter has sought to show that, despite continuing pressures throughout the advanced economies for the use of a particular model (the 'new managerialism') to ensure 'efficiency' of service delivery in public services, its adoption does not automatically ensure success. Some of the difficulties involved in using accounting techniques to achieve enhanced control have been highlighted above. The general picture presented is that of a cautious approach to costing and devolved budgets in the face of pressures to give a new, high profile visibility to accounting. This cautious approach fits well with the realities of achieving organisational change in public services where there exists a dominant, embedded (entrenched?) set of values. Indeed, there is evidence that such values have placed boundaries around or constrained the wider development of devolved budgets. This issue – of the manner in which accounting technologies, such as devolved budgets, sit within the organisational, and even societal, context – can be seen as being of fundamental importance to the organisation, as a whole. Examples of the manner in which there are interactions between the organisation and its external environment have been cited above. Others include further boundary issues (the shifting of organisational costs to informal carers) transitional effects (e.g. from 1 April 1993 high levels of residents had 'protected status'); the difficulty of forecasting because of the problems of identifying care needs, (with consequent difficulty over the 'level of spend'); and all of this in a situation in which budgets have been incompletely devolved. Given these complexities, it is not surprising that the story of the role of costs and budgets within social care remains an unfolding one, which merits further, closer analysis fully to understand its implications.

Acknowledgements

The author wishes to acknowledge the use of data from ESRC-sponsored project (R000221128), Markets and Choices: Contracts for Care, as part of this paper.

References

Anthony, R. and Herzlinger, R. (1980) *Management Control in Non-Profit Organisations* (Revised edition). Homewood, Illinois: R.D. Irwin.

Bland, R., Bland, R., Cheetham, J., Lapsley, I. and Llewellyn, S. (1992) *Residential Homes for Elderly People: Their Costs and Quality.* Edinburgh: HMSO.

Brunsson, N. (1994) 'Politicization and company-ization – on institutional affiliation and confusion in the organizational world.' *Management Accounting Research 5,* 3,4, 323–336.

Hood, C. (1991) 'A public management for all seasons?' *Public Administration* 69, 3–19.

Lapsley, I. and Llewellyn, S. (1994) Markets and Choices: Contracts for Care, End of Award Report, (Research grant R00022128), Economic and Social Research Council.

Mintzberg, H. (1975) *Impediments to the Use of Management Information*. New York: National Association of Accountants.

Stalker, K., Taylor. J., and Petch. A. (1994) *Implementing Community Care in Scotland: Early Snapshots*. Community Care in Scotland Discussion Paper No 4. Stirling: Social Work Research Centre, University of Stirling.

Chapter 8

Costing Care Needs For Disabled People
An Accounting Approach

Margaret King and Sue Llewellyn

The introduction of community care legislation on 1st April 1993 was, in many ways, the most significant social policy initiative for decades. It posed, and will continue to pose, challenges for financial, professional and organisational agendas as the boundaries around institutional care and care in the community are redrawn. Care management, contract setting and an increasing policy emphasis on the more explicit matching of needs and resources are all areas where financial, professional and organisational issues are intertwined. Considerable work with both people and information systems will be needed before such issues are resolved.

This chapter primarily addresses the financial area – specifically it outlines the methods and results of a research project which built up cost profiles for a number of severely disabled people (with varying levels of need) who are currently accommodated in a residential setting. Such a project has immediate relevance under the new community care regime as provider units now receive funding from the local authorities on a contract basis. These funding arrangements require more detailed financial information than was previously necessary. Aggregate organisational budgets permitted the calculation of average costs. However, the use of average costs in striking contracts would mask the differing cost consequences which flow from the differential demands on resources made by clients whose needs span a spectrum of physical dependencies. As contract setting becomes more sophisticated – moving from a block basis through to cost and volume (and in some cases individual) specifications – individual costs become necessary in order to be able to base prices on realistic cost information and to avoid cross-subsidisation between clients. In addition to this immediate practical relevance, the project findings also allow some exploration of the broader issues at stake. First, the scrutiny of the relationship between assessed needs and associated costs should allow for better resource management in matching needs and resources (both in contract negotiation and in the monitoring of service delivery). Second, more refined cost information will permit more informed assessments of the cost-effectiveness of residential care *vis-à-vis* care in the community. Third, the availability of more accurate and detailed costs can assist provider units in planning service developments (e.g., in deciding in whether to offer 'outreach' or community services).

The Project

The project consisted of detailed case studies at two different research settings. This chapter concentrates on the first of these settings – Upper Springland, a purpose built residential establishment administered by the Scottish Council for Spastics (to be renamed 'Capability, Scotland' in Spring 1996). This unit is sophisticated in terms of the facilities it houses and the services it offers. It has a wide range of facilities: a number of flatlets; a community centre incorporating a theatre and recreational area; a respite unit; a day centre; a skill centre; and a hydrotherapy pool and gymnasium. The central aims of the project were, first, to build up needs assessments for a selected sample of the current residents, second, to construct the costs incurred in meeting these needs and third, to examine both data sets in order to draw out any underlying relationships between clients' needs profiles and their associated costs. *Prima facie*, it was expected that the greater the level of the client's needs and the greater the degree of complexity of such needs the greater would be the associated costs in terms of the care delivered. Three dimensions of need were defined for the purposes of the study: physical disability, need for emotional/social support and need for help with self-management skills. It was envisaged that information on needs and costs would be pivotal to contract setting. In addition, the study setting allowed the investigation of three other broad areas for which contract specifications may be drawn up: the type of facilities offered, the range of disabilities (or client mix) which can be accommodated and the time span of the care provided (specifically whether the client is expected to remain within the centre for an indefinite period or whether a shorter stay followed by a return to the wider community is planned).

The research setting
Upper Springland offers care to some 60 disabled persons whose disabilities cover cerebral palsy, brain injury (mostly following road accidents) and a number of degenerative conditions. The staff at the unit cannot directly alleviate the disadvantage imposed by these circumstances – they rather address the profound physical, social and emotional needs which are consequent upon these medical conditions (Smith and O'Hara 1992). The ethos of Upper Springland places an emphasis on independence and choice and residents are expected to exercise judgement in making their needs known to staff. Rigid routines are avoided and much effort has been put into creating a stimulating environment – the skill centre offers opportunities for education and the pursuit of interests while the theatre, pool and gymnasium are designed for recreational and therapeutic activities.

The research methods

Twenty-five residents were selected for the study. As the research was intended to elicit clients' needs and associated costs across a continuum of disability a classification scheme was established from which a sample of clients was chosen. With the help of the staff at the site, a preliminary assessment of residents was made along two dimensions: degree of need for physical care and degree of need for social/emotional support. Table 8.1 shows the initial allocation of residents at the site with the figures in brackets representing the actual sample.

Table 8.1 Allocation of residents by degree of need for help with daily self-care

Emotional/Social Self-Sufficiency	Total Care	Lot of Help	Limited Help	No Routine Help
Good				
OK	9(5)	1	2(2)	3(2)
Not Good	12(5)	16(6)	11(5)	

Residents were free to refuse to take part and, in the event, six declined. Each of these people was replaced by someone else from within the same category of perceived need (wherever this was possible).

Needs assessment

The Barthel Index was used in this study as an instrument to measure residents' physical dependency. This index was devised by Mahoney and Barthel (1965) for use in measuring levels of self-care and mobility in the physically impaired. It has subsequently been used by Granger, Albricht and Hamilton (1979) in assessing the outcomes of medical rehabilitation programmes for severely disabled people. The index identifies nine areas of self-care, including sphincter-control, and six areas of mobility. Each of these factors was scored on the basis of 'independent' (either with or without some artificial aid); 'needs help' and 'dependent'. The nine self-care functions have a maximum total score of 53, and the mobility functions have a maximum total score of 47. Thus the total Barthel score can range from zero (total dependence) to 100 (complete independence).

The residents' self-management skills were assessed in the following areas: laundry, housework, cooking, shopping, telephone, health care visits, and finance; and were scored according to whether residents were able to undertake these tasks, whether residents could only undertake them with help or whether residents were unable but took responsibility for the tasks.

During the course of the interviews involving the Barthel Index and the assessment of self-management skills residents were also asked about the number and quality of relationships they have with various groups of people – family, friends in the community (or in the unit) and staff. This provided a measure of the extent of the residents' social network. Questions were also asked about whether the residents were satisfied with their lives, whether they felt they coped, whether they were cheerful or felt 'down', and whether they were lonely or worried much. These questions and the overall response of residents in the interviews, along with the results of interviews with staff, enabled an assessment to be made of the residents' emotional states and the extent of their social networks.

Constructing costs

In building up costs there was a primary focus on staff time spent in caring for residents. Such time was recorded by means of diaries. In these diaries activities were split into three categories: the time spent helping residents with physical tasks such as eating or bathing; the time spent assisting residents with self-management tasks such as laundry and the time spent talking to or counselling residents. In addition to these diaries, which were kept for one week, records were also kept over a four week period of the use made of the physiotherapy department and of the skill centre. Cost information to be attached to this activity data was obtained from the detailed 1993–94 budget for each of the units and from information on rates of pay and staff hours. An amount for imputed depreciation was added to the budget figure (since depreciation was not included in the budget). The depreciation was calculated on the basis of insurance values (no historical cost data being available), with buildings being depreciated at two per cent·per annum and contents/equipment at twenty per cent per annum.

Costs were dealt with first by allocation to designated cost centres and then absorption to individuals by use of an overhead recovery rate. Within this framework budgeted costs were attached to individual residents by means of a multi-stage process, as detailed below.

(1) Ten cost centres were identified – the skill centre, physiotherapy, administration and management, transport, catering, housekeeping/maintenance (referred to as 'support' cost centres), and the four residential units. Budgeted costs were clearly identified as relating to specific cost centres due to their nature (e.g. cleaning materials).

(2) Costs were re-allocated from the support cost centres to the units. Administration and management and transport costs were allocated across the residential units, the skill centre and physiotherapy on the basis of the staff cost in each. Catering costs and housekeeping/maintenance costs were allocated across the four residential units on the basis of the number of residents in each. The rationale behind this was that all six cost centres (the residential units, the skill centre and physiotherapy) make demands on administration and transport whereas only the residential units make use of catering and housekeeping.

(3) The 'direct' staff cost, defined as being the cost of the direct contact time between staff and residents, was calculated as shown in Table 8.2.

Table 8.2 Calculation of direct staff cost

(i)   Total staff time was available from the budget which showed a breakdown of individual hourly salaries and hours worked.

(ii)   Contact time was derived from the diaries summing the time spent with each of the 25 residents in the sample, excluding physiotherapy and skill centre time, and multiplying by 60/25* to give an estimated amount of time spent with all residents over a week.

(iii)   Comparing this to the total weekly hours gave a figure of 37% of staff time being direct contact time. 37% of staff cost in the units was therefore classed as direct cost, the remaining 63% being treated, along with the other costs, as overhead.

(iv)   The direct staff cost was attached to the activity information by costing each period of contact at the hourly pay rate of the member(s) of staff involved.

* 60 residents in total

(4)   Overhead for the residential units was treated in two ways depending on the nature of the cost: variable costs (hereafter referred to as 'overheads') (see Table 8.3) were allocated per direct contact hour. Dividing total cost in this category by total contact hours gave an overhead recovery rate of £12 per direct contact hour. Fixed costs were allocated (see Table 8.3) as a standing charge at a flat rate per resident per week, reflecting that the use of these costs was not directly related to the amount of staff help received by the resident. Dividing these costs by the number of resident weeks in the year (cost/(60*52)) resulted in a rate of £332 per resident per week.

(5)   Physiotherapy costs were dealt with in a similar way, with direct staff time being costed at the hourly pay rate. The non-direct element of physiotherapy salary was then allocated across the four residential units to reflect the fact that all residents have 'on call' access to the physiotherapist for advice or help. Non-salary physiotherapy overhead was allocated to those using the physiotherapy service per direct physiotherapy hour. Overhead/direct hours gave a rate of £23 per direct hour. Since

Table 8.3 Overhead costs – Upper Springland

Costs allocated per contact hour	Costs included in the standing charge
Non-direct wages and salaries	Residents' clothing allowance
National insurance costs	Catering cost
Pension costs	Housekeeping and maintenance cost
Sleeping in allowance	
Overtime	Administration and management costs
Sickness/maternity payments	
Staff travel	Transport costs
Staff training	Imputed depreciation cost
Cost of living allowance	Physiotherapy cost (non-direct
Protective clothing	staff cost)

some of the people using the physiotherapy service are day attenders rather than residents at Upper Springland, some of the physiotherapy cost will be recovered only as it is charged to day attenders. For the purposes of this exercise it has been assumed that costs will be charged to day attenders on the same basis as they are to residents. An alternative would be to charge a marginal cost, but average cost is used here on the grounds that day attenders make use of and benefit from the same facilities and services as do residents.

(6) Skill centre costs were treated differently from the other costs. Data was collected on use of the skill centre over a period of four weeks by use of a 'register'. Annual skill centre cost was divided by 13 to give the cost of a four-week period – thus matching the period for which activity data were gathered. The cost was allocated to individual activities on the basis of the proportion of total activity time in the four weeks which they represented. The cost per activity was then divided by the number of participants over the four-week period to give a cost per participant per session. This was then attached to individual residents on the basis of usage as

recorded by the diaries. Again, the skill centre is used by day attenders as well as by residents. Consequently, some of the skill centre cost (around 37%) will only be recovered by charges for day attenders. It has been assumed once again that day attendance charges for the skill centre would be on the same basis as charges for residents' use of the skill centre.

The research results

The Barthel Index gives an assessment of self care and mobility. The total ranging from 0–100 is an indication of the individual's level of dependency. A high score indicates a high level of independence and a low score a high degree of dependence. Specifically, a score of 60 or under represents a person who is severely dependent; 50 or under represents someone who is very severely dependent. The index is made up of two parts – self-care (with possible scores of 0–53) and mobility (with possible scores of 0–47). Total Barthel scores for residents in the sample ranged from 15 (highly dependent) to 90 (highly independent), reflecting a wide range of physical dependence/independence and hence of need for help with daily self-care. The mean score was 57. Self-care scores ranged from 15 to 53, with two residents scoring the maximum possible score of 53. The average self-care score was 40. Mobility scores for the residents in the sample ranged from 0 (five residents) to 42 (the maximum possible score was 47). The average mobility score was 18. For self-managing skills of the residents included in the study ten had 'good' self-management skills, twelve were classed 'acceptable' and only three had 'not good' or poor self-management skills. This may be a reflection of Upper Springland's policy of encouraging residents to take responsibility for a task even if they are unable to physically perform it. For social self-sufficiency, nine residents were classified as 'good', ten as 'acceptable' and six had 'not good' or poor social self-sufficiency. For emotional self-sufficiency nine Residents, were classified as 'good', ten were 'acceptable' and six 'not good'. Seven of those falling in the 'good' category also had a good social network.

Costs

The result of attaching costs to the activity data gathered by the diaries was to build up a cost per person per week for each individual resident in the study. These costs were split into the cost of staff time, overhead for care staff or physiotherapy and skill centre cost. A total cost was obtained which includes the weekly standing charge of £332 per resident.

In order to try and establish some relationship between cost and type of need, costs (excluding the weekly overhead charge) were split over the three activity areas: physical help, help with self-management skills (including the cost of time spent in the skill centre) and the cost of time spent in social interaction with the resident.[1] Time spent in each of these types of activities was identified from the description of each activity given in the staff contact diary.[2] A summary of the results of the costing exercise is given in Table 8.4.

Table 8.4 Summary of the cost analysis

N=25	Physical cost	Management cost	Social interaction cost	Standing charge	Grand total
Mean cost	£136	£97	£44	£332	£609
Range	£3 –£504	£3 –£313	£2 –£254	–	£336 –£1116
Standard deviation	£144	£86	£57	–	£239

Table 8.4 shows that, apart from the weekly standing charge, the largest, and also the most variable, element of cost is the cost of physical care. The average physical care cost is £136 per week (including both staff cost and variable overhead) but this ranges from £3 (very little time spent helping with physical care tasks) to £504 (representing a high level of staff input to meet the physical needs of the resident). Self-management and social interaction costs also vary widely.

---

1 Social interaction time does not include periods when the primary activity was a physical or self-management task, though it is likely that staff and residents also use this as social interaction time.

2 There were four individuals who had zero costs for social and emotional interaction; two of these also had zero costs for help with self-management tasks. These people had relatively good communication skills and, hence, were able to form relationships with other residents. Therefore they were less demanding on staff time and conversations with staff were of very short duration. The further implications of the cost consequences of communication skills are explored later in this chapter.

The links between needs and costs

To establish whether or not there was a link between assessed needs and costs, possible relationships were explored in three areas. First, physical care costs were related to the level of physical help required, second, self-management costs to the scores for management skills and third, social interaction costs to the scores for emotional and social self-sufficiency.

The most significant findings were those relating to physical care. As Table 8.5 shows, average costs were markedly different between the four different levels of assessed need.

The relationship between average cost and need for help with daily physical care is ás expected since more help involves more staff time and

Table 8.5 Average weekly physical care costs related to degree of need for help with daily self-care

	Total care (Score: 0–50)	Lot of help (Score: 51–60)	Limited help (Score: 61–85)	No routine help (Score: 86–100)
Average cost	£289	£87	£26	£10
Range	£105 – £504	£47 – £181	£10 – £67	£3 – £14

thus incurs more staff cost and more labour related overhead.

The most striking difference on average costs is that between the 'total care' and 'lot of help' categories. Average costs for residents who require 'total care' is £289 as compared to £87 for residents who need a 'lot of help'. It was, therefore, concluded that a 'Barthel break' occurred at a Barthel score of 50. Clients whose needs assessments indicated Barthel scores of 50 or below could be expected to be, on average, roughly three times as costly as clients whose Barthel scores were above 50.

Average weekly costs for help with self-management tasks also varied as expected with the scores for self-management self-sufficiency. However as Table 8.6 shows there were wide variations in the cost of providing help with self-management skills within each of the categories.

Closer examination of the data revealed that the wide variability within each of the categories was related primarily to the differences in the residents' abilities to speak. Residents who were able to communicate

Table 8.6 Average weekly costs of self-management help related to self-managing skills

	Managing self-sufficiency Good	Managing self-sufficiency OK	Managing self-sufficiency Not good
Average cost	£90	£83	£178
Range	£19 – £209	£3 – £309	£72 – £313

were able to make their own telephone calls or even go shopping by themselves. In contrast, residents who had to write in order to communicate or who were reliant on aids such as Bliss boards, incurred much more substantial costs, due to the staff time devoted to communicating on their behalf. Also of significance for self-managing skills was the ability to use the upper body, especially arms and hands – such ability greatly enhanced residents' self-sufficiency.

When average weekly social interaction costs were related to social self-sufficiency scores no discernible pattern emerged (see Table 8.7).

Table 8.7 Average weekly social interaction costs related to social self-sufficiency

	Social self-sufficiency good	Social self-sufficiency OK	Social self-sufficiency not good
Average cost	£65	£18	£54
Range	£9 – £254	£2 – £53	£7 – £117

These results did not point to a relationship between clients' need for social support and staff time devoted in a response to it. However, for several reasons, the identification of social interaction costs was difficult. First, the costs presented above represent the staff time costs over and above that time spent in conversation and counselling whilst physical or management care tasks were taking place. Second, it is possible that staff time (and hence costs) spent talking with a particular resident is not dependent so much on a need for this type of contact as on the relationship between the resident and staff. Staff may seek out those residents whose company they enjoy and spend less time with those who are less socially skilled or, as with self-management skills, residents' abilities to speak may be a factor which is making for a complex pattern here. Third, the research instrument may not have been sufficiently sensitive to adequately reflect the degree of clients' need for social support.

Relating average weekly social interaction costs to emotional self-sufficiency again yielded equivocal results, as shown below in Table 8.8.

Table 8.8 Average weekly social interaction costs related to emotional self-sufficiency

	Emotional self-sufficiency good	Emotional self-sufficiency OK	Emotional self-sufficiency not good
Average cost	£26	£69	£28
Range	£7 – £75	£2 – £254	£9 – £117

The conclusion reached on the results of relating social interaction costs to emotional self-sufficiency must be similar to those reached over social self-sufficiency.

Discussion and conclusions

On the relationship between needs and cost

When relationships between needs and costs were examined the strongest connections emerged between the degree of clients' physical dependence and the level of resource (in terms of staff time) required to meet those needs. Particularly striking was the very high resource input needed to care for those clients whose Barthel scores fell below 50 – this finding led to the conclusion that there was a 'Barthel break' at the 50 mark which had very significant resource consequences. However, a greater degree of complexity to this pattern emerged when the two Barthel sub-scores (on self-care and mobility) were examined. Lack of mobility was a less significant factor both in its cost consequences, and in its impact upon the residents' ability to live independently, than was a high degree of dependency in need for self-care. This followed as an inability to walk could be compensated for by the use of an electric wheelchair. Where residents were unable to propel their own wheelchairs there were minor cost consequences but such clients were usually already more costly as they tended to have low scores for other self-care tasks. A further complication to the conclusion that low Barthel scores will inevitably have significant cost consequences relates to clients' ability to communicate. Where clients, although severely physically disabled, are able to speak and express themselves confidently, demands on staff time are likely to be less. Such clients are able to take responsibility for tasks even if they cannot physically undertake the tasks. For example, shopping and organising health-care visits can be done by telephone. In the area of self-management skills the ability to use arms and hands also reduced clients' need for staff help.

On the costs incurred in meeting social/emotional needs no obvious unidimensional relationship was observed. A complex interplay of factors is at work here and more sensitive research instruments and more in-depth investigation will be necessary to order to tease out relationships. Work in this area is particularly relevant, due to the changing nature of referrals to Upper Springland. The unit was originally intended to offer permanent accommodation for clients who were quite severely physically disabled but who were socially and emotionally relatively self-sufficient. This situation is, however, changing – an increasing proportion of residents have additional difficulties – such as a long history of institutionalisation, borderline mental handicap, epilepsy, emotional instability or behavioral problems (Goodall 1989). This research confirmed these observations. Only nine of the twenty-five residents interviewed had 'good' social networks and, again, only nine were thought to have a 'good' level of emotional self-sufficiency. The staff's intuitive original classification of residents, based upon working with them, indicated an even greater need for emotional and social support at the unit. Staff did not feel that any residents were 'good' in terms of emotional/social self-sufficiency. They assessed nine of the sample as being 'OK' and sixteen as being 'not good'. Clearly, under these circumstances of an increasing proportion of clients with social and emotional needs, and a staff concern and commitment to support these needs (whether in-house or through external referrals for counselling and/or psychological support) further indications of the cost consequences of meeting these needs would be most beneficial. The research study has made available the costs incurred in meeting individual clients' social and emotional needs but more refined data would be necessary to assess the cost implications of a client mix which encompassed a high proportion of clients with profound social and emotional difficulties.

Implications for management

The increasing emphasis on community care has had the effect of high-lighting the nature of organisational objectives within residential units, such as Upper Springland. Of particular interest, at the moment, are the co-existing (or perhaps competing) objectives of the 'home for life' approach with its concomitant caring values and an ethos which seeks to maximise independence through encouraging self-help (with a return to the community as a possible outcome). Co-existing organisational value systems can invoke tensions. Goodall (1989) refers to the conflict between '... the ideal of providing a setting where disabled people could be enabled to live "normal" lives and the approach to residents as clients, who ought to be helped to change in certain ways assumed to be beneficial' (p.133). These issues are relevant in decisions on the scope and detail required to cost a more 'enabling' role for Upper Springland. Such a role would place greater emphasis on developing clients' potential for social and emotional independence. This role would carry with it greater demands for infor-mation on the cost implications of such developments.

On admissions policy the use of the 'Barthel break' will provide useful information on the cost implications of the very severely physically disabled. The index should also be helpful in planning staffing require-ments in terms of numbers, expertise, availability and flexibility.

The research highlighted the additional resources (in terms of staff time) required to meet clients' communication problems. Such findings imply that more cost effective ways of enhancing clients' abilities to speak may well be available. The upgrading of speech aids and more extensive use of speech therapy (supplemented by staff training programmes) may have long-term cost benefits.

In terms of cost recovery policies management may wish to have available a three tier cost structure. A standing charge would indicate the level of resource needed to recover fixed overheads. The standing charge plus the costs of care would give a minimum charge. This minimum charge could be pitched at different levels, derived from clients' Barthel scores. Thus individuals with a Barthel score of more than 70 would incur a charge of £X with those having scores of between 50 and 70 incurring charges of £X+Y and so on. The research data indicates an exponential rather than an incremental charging policy (i.e. one which recognises the heavy demands on staff time made by the very severely physically disabled).

Implications for contract setting

The research demonstrated that it is possible to cost care for individuals, but such an exercise is time-consuming and, therefore, costly to implement. It may, however, be possible for provider units to repeat the present study at further points in order to update the costings. The need for such updates would depend upon any changing needs of the present client group or on a changing client mix. The further development of cost classification schemes based on the differing resource inputs required by different client groups is indicated. The Barthel Index can form the basis of one such scheme but, at present, the resource implications of differing levels of social/emotional needs are unclear.

The wide range of costs observed (£336 to £1,116 per resident week) implies that a high degree of cross-subsidisation is inevitable when block contracts are used. However, the difficulties (referred to above) attached to individual costings imply that, at present, some form of cost and volume contract will be optimal. Such an approach would result in specifically tailored contracts for cases which vary significantly from the average without the need to negotiate individual contracts for 'middle-range' cases. However, the concept of the 'average' client presents particular difficulties in the area of the severely physically disabled. The wide range of physical disabilities, the number of different medical conditions present in the client group and the quite profound social and emotional needs of clients makes the identification of 'average' cases very problematic. In terms of costs (and hence prices) for contracts the wide range of disability and associated need in this client group raises the issue of which care needs will be considered 'basic' and which will be thought of as incurring additional expenditure. Speech therapy or psychological counselling, for example, may be pivotal in enhancing a resident's independence and in reducing an experienced sense of marginal identity, but considerable flexibility will be required in order for contract setting to encompass the wide range of potential additional facilities and services needed by this client group. A comparison with, for example, elderly people in residential care, reveals the heterogeneity of needs (and hence costs) of the severely physically disabled.

Provider units, such as Upper Springland, offer a highly specialised service to a distinct client group; therefore, they will often be the sole such unit within quite a wide geographical area. Hence, in the past, the cross subsidisation associated with a block contract with a single purchaser, (commonly a regional authority), has not posed any pressing problems. However, there are a number of pragmatic considerations over the continuing use of block contracts. An emphasis on care in the community will soon result in fewer referrals from within the region in which the unit is situated and an increased number of referrals from more remote areas. When the unit is contracting with a greater number of purchasers, cross-subsidisation is likely to become more of an issue. In addition, an expectation that an increasing number of clients will remain in the community will raise doubts in the minds of purchasers over whether they will fill all the vacancies purchased on a 'block' basis. Also, the continuing implementation of community care will result in a blurring of the boundaries between residential care and domiciliary care. It is likely that within provider units, such as Upper Springland, there will be an increased emphasis on programmed respite care and outreach services will become much more prevalent. Hence, there is an expectation that patterns of service provision will become much more complex.

Other contract issues are raised over charging for vacant rooms where clients are hospitalised for a period, and, charging for clients whose needs profiles may change significantly over time. Provider units would, at least, wish to cover fixed overheads where clients are hospitalised. The uncertainties attached to the long-term resource implications of clients with, for example, multiple sclerosis pose difficulties for contract setting. Providers would be greatly assisted in such cases by provision for reviewing costs at intervals. Some element of retrospective charging (to supplement prospective contracts) is indicated where clients with conditions such as multiple sclerosis follow protracted patterns of relapse and remission.

This research has used an accounting perspective to approach the difficult and complex task of costing care for people with profound physical disabilities. Disability connotes need and the research has demonstrated some of the resource implications of meeting such need. It is hoped that this information will be of benefit in the continuing work of provider units such as Upper Springland both in negotiating contracts and in resource management.

Acknowledgement

This research was sponsored by the Scottish Council for Spastics, the Scottish Trust for the Physically Disabled and the Social Work Services Group of the Scottish Office.

References

Brand, E., King, M., Lapsley I. and Llewellyn S. (1995) *The Costs and Quality of Care for People with Disabilities*. Edinburgh: Central Research Unit, Scottish Office.

Goodall J. (1989) 'Residential homes for physically disabled adults: Lessons from the present and potential for the future.' In L. Barton (ed) *Integration: Myth or Reality.* London: The Falmer Press.

Granger C.U., Albricht G. and Hamilton B. (1979) 'Outcome of comprehensive medical rehabilitations: measurement by pulses and Barthel Index.' *Archives of Physical Rehabilitation 60*, 145–154.

Mahoney F.L. and Barthel D.W. (1965) 'Functional evaluation: The Barthel index.' *Maryland State Medical Journal, February 1965*, 61–65.

Smith G. and O'Hara P. (1992) 'Managing social services in the 1990s.' In L. Willcocks and J. Harrow (eds) *Rediscovering Public Services Management.* Maidenhead: McGraw-Hill.

Chapter 9

The Costs of Informal Care

Ann Netten

Introduction

The current policy drive is overwhelmingly towards efficiency both in the public sector as a whole and health and social services in particular. Within this the objective of achieving 'value for money' is being approached primarily by making decision makers aware of the cost implication of their decisions. Thus where there are two equally appropriate ways of achieving a given objective, awareness of the costs facilitates the use of the cheaper option. As a consequence considerable attention is being focused on establishing the costs of community care services (Beecham and Netten 1993). But there is an important gap in cost information, concerning the costs to those who provide the majority of care: individuals in the informal sector.

The problems associated with adopting a single agency perspective in achieving value for money or simply minimizing costs were highlighted by the Audit Commission (1986). They identified the perverse incentive toward inefficient use of resources stemming from the use of Department of Social Security funds to maintain elderly people in residential care while local authorities bore the cost of community care services. The reforms introduced by the NHS and Community Care Act, 1990, giving local authorities responsibility for purchasing public funded social care, go some way to rectify these problems. But local authorities' lack of awareness of, and responsibility for, the cost of health and informal care limit the potential to make the most efficient use of society's resources in providing care.

Problems of inefficiency are most acute where the costs of achieving a goal, such as providing care, are borne by different agencies or sectors. Although there are areas of overlap, health services are for the most part complements to personal social services so there are limits to the degree to which costs can be shifted across sectors. Moreover, the joint planning process provides a mechanism for resolving problems of overlap. Social service provision, on the other hand, is a direct substitute for the informal sector, whose members are handicapped by a lack of hard information about costs or a coherent voice in the policy process.

While policies aimed at diverting people from residential care to care in their own homes will probably reduce the costs to the health and social services, almost certainly they will increase the cost to 'the community'. Recognition of this fact is implicit in the increased policy emphasis on supporting carers (*Caring for People* 1989). But policies about the role of carers and the informal sector as a whole tend to be vague and ill-defined (Twigg and Atkin 1993a). Partly this is due to the fact that there is so little information about the costs to carers. Much work has been done on who does the caring (Finch and Groves 1983, Qureshi and Walker 1989), experiences of the caring process (Ungerson 1987) and particular problems associated with conditions such as dementia (Levin, Sinclair and Gorbach 1989). Informal sector issues have been discussed in terms of the stress on carers (Charnley 1989), needs for services (Twigg, Atkin and Perring 1990), equity (Finch and Groves 1983) or concerns about the future supply of carers (Phillipson and Walker 1986). Underlying each of these is the issue of the opportunity cost of informal care, both to carers and to society as a whole.

In this chapter the theoretical issues in the costing of this unpaid contribution are identified and the methodological implications of estimating costs to society or to individual carers are identified. An application of the approach is described which costs the informal care input from the principal carer in a study of elderly people receiving community based social care in ten local authorities (Davies *et al.* 1990). Before it is possible to cost anything, however, it is of vital importance to be clear what it is that is being costed: exactly what is meant by informal care?

Defining informal care

When clarifying exactly what is meant by informal care it is helpful to use the social production of welfare approach (Netten and Davies 1990, Netten 1993) in which the household is depicted as a productive unit with the household members aiming to derive welfare from time and goods by producing commodities such as housework and nutrition. The ability of the household to produce these is subject to a number of restrictions among which is concern for the welfare of other household and family members.

Care is required when disability results in an increased demand for commodities and/or a lowered productivity level from one person to the point where another member has to substitute for them or other changes need to be made in the way commodities are produced. For example if someone breaks a leg the majority of their household chores will be taken over by another member of the household. A diagnosis of diabetes however, may result in no substitution but an increased amount of expenditure and work associated with the production of the commodity of nutrition.

Normally, the need for informal care will be due to a short term situation, such as illness, which the household will easily meet within its own resources. Long term progressive disability that tends to occur in later life, however, can put intolerable burdens on a household which has limited resources. It is in such situations that members of other households become involved in producing commodities for the person with disabilities and the productive unit becomes the informal care network.

Types of cost

Using this framework in costing the impact of disability on an individual carer or on society it is necessary to define what has been given up in order to change the way commodities are produced as a consequence of disability. The importance of establishing comprehensive costs is paramount in this process as costs are to a degree substitutable. For example, in ensuring that an elderly person with disability has an adequate level of 'housework' a carer may pay for someone to do the cleaning or go to the elderly person's house and do it him or herself. In the first case money has been given up, in the latter time. Similarly, the opportunity cost associated with providing care to somebody in a different households may be such that an elderly person moves into a carer's home. Space and privacy have been lost but less time will need to be spent travelling and cleaning another house.

The types of cost shown in Table 9.1 are used as examples of situations for the carer which have different cost implications. Obviously not all carers will incur all of these types of cost, but they help to specify what needs to be taken into consideration when costing care provided by carers in different situations.

Table 9.1 Types of costs of care

I	Direct financial expenditure on goods and services
II	Carer gives up non-waged time
III	Carer gives up waged time
IV	Carer gives up future prospects
V	Carer gives up accommodation

Having identified what has been given up it is necessary to put a value on it. It is the result of what has been given up, for example time, rather than the time itself that needs to be valued. Benefit or pleasure gained from the time spent doing an activity (e.g. housework) is defined as direct utility. Indirect utility is the benefit that results from the activity (a clean house). Services are always costed on the basis of lost indirect utility – the value of labour in terms of the wage rate and so on, as a financial cost can be attached to this. Similarly, the lost indirect utility will be identified as the cost to carers in the following analysis.

Although the cost to the carer as well as the cost to society is discussed here, it is society's valuation that is used in both cases. The value that each person puts on his or her time (or money) will be individually determined. How carers feel about what they have given up can be explored through the relationship between the 'objective' opportunity cost, which uses prices determined in the market place, choices made in practice and subjective feelings, measured by such indicators as the malaise inventory (Rutter, Tizard and Whitmore 1970).

Direct financial expenditure

The financial costs of care include consumable goods and services that would not have been purchased in the absence of disability. These will include such costs as increased heating bills, laundry, special foods and the cost of travel when visiting an elderly person in order to look after them. The cash valuation of these provides the estimate of indirect utility or opportunity cost.

There are two principal types of goods – consumption and capital. Consumption goods are consumed or used up in the process of production. Capital goods are manufactured goods that are used to produce. In the household context expenditure on capital goods might include adaptations such as ramps or aids such as button fasteners which increase a disabled person's productivity.

Actual expenditure on food, heating and laundry which is attributable to disability is often hard to establish in practice. It requires detailed questions about expenditure patterns and a base line for comparison, be it other households in similar circumstances without the disability in question or speculations by the members of the household concerned about likely expenditure in the absences of disability. In particular, problems arise because of the effect of disability on income. Disability can result in loss of income, so in households where there is disability, expenditure on such items as food and fuel will often be lower than in households where there is no disability.

Baldwin (1985) investigated the financial consequences of disablement in children by comparing the expenditure patterns in families with disabled children with those in the same income bands in the Family Expenditure Survey. Where information about actual levels of expenditure is not forthcoming it is necessary to draw on this type of study or to use other indicators such as the supplementary benefit payments for the type of additional expense which has been identified such as heating or dietary needs. It was necessary to adopt this type of approach in the application described at the end of this chapter.

Household 'capital' goods include aids such as wheelchairs and adaptations such as stair lifts. In order to assess their cost, allowance should be made for the fact that they depreciate over time. Expenditure on capital goods ought therefore to be discounted over the expected life of the items.

An alternative approach to the problem of assessing the cost of disability is the derivation of household equivalence scales. Equivalence scales are used to gauge the impact of, for example, an additional child on a family's standard of living. They are estimated on the basis of establishing how much additional expenditure would be required in order to bring a household up to the standard of living it would have had in the absence of the child. Jones and O'Donnell (1992) use the household production approach to examine the impact of disability on expenditure in households where there are younger adults with disabilities. They draw on approaches described by Deaton and Muellbauer (1980) distinguishing expenditure on items that are affected by disability and items that are not. The level or share of expenditure on those goods which are not affected by disability are used as a proxy for standard of living. While clearly potentially extremely useful this type of approach is complex and often requires more in the way of reliable data than is available in practice. In particular, transactions between households can not be dealt with using Family Expenditure Survey data.

In estimating the social opportunity cost of care, financial transactions between individuals or households will be irrelevant. In the case of the costs to the carer, however, the transactions both financial and in terms of goods will be relevant. Indeed the carer may end up financially better off because of a caring relationship.

Costing time

The bulk of the cost of informal care is in terms of a commitment of time, so how this is costed is of fundamental importance. There are two distinct problems in costing time foregone. The first is estimating the time spent because of care. The second is identifying how this time should be costed.

Estimating time spent on care

One difficulty that arises when identifying opportunity cost of time is that, given the relationship between a person with disability and a carer prior to the onset of disability, a certain amount of time would probably have been spent together in the absence of disability. This time cannot be regarded as part of the opportunity cost. One assumption could be that only time spent on caring tasks should be included. But where mobility difficulties result in isolation a vital element of the caring relationship is the social contact provided which is an integral part of the care.

Where carers live in separate households it is sometimes possible to establish likely contact time in the absence of disability by discussing prior visiting patterns. Such patterns are likely to vary enormously depending on the relationship between the people concerned, cultural norms and so on.

Where a carer and an elderly person share a household, joint production becomes an issue in addition to the problem of separating out 'normal' levels of social contact. Joint production occurs when more than one commodity is produced at once: for instance having a chat (social contact) while doing the housework. If there is no loss of productivity the case is clear: there is no measurable cost in terms of indirect utility as there has been no effective substitution. No time has been given up in order to produce the additional commodity of social contact. A cost is incurred if the distraction or irritation caused by this results in lost productivity. This can only be effectively costed if it is possible to ascertain how much extra time would be needed to achieve the same level of production. For the purposes of estimation it is often reasonable to assume that where carers and elderly people live in the same household time spent on social interaction need not result in any specific substitution of time. Caring tasks, on the other hand, normally will result in time being given up. Moreover, carers often can be quite clear that considerations of safety, while not resulting in any specific tasks, mean they cannot leave an elderly person alone and thus have spent time in the company of the elderly person that otherwise would have been spent elsewhere.

In empirical studies another difficulty may emerge. Often the last visit made is not seen as typical but carers find it impossible to estimate what is typical. In the majority of cases substituting time spent on caring during the last visit is a reasonable compromise, but this can result in no time apparently being spent on caring tasks while caring tasks are identified as being carried out for the elderly person.

In a study of ten local authorities (Davies *et al.* 1990) these cases were examined in detail and it emerged that the tasks concerned were: shopping, collecting pensions, accompanying the person out, medication, odd jobs about the house, laundry and gardening. It can be argued that because the carer would have to be shopping anyway, relatively little extra time would have to be spent on these activities, although this will clearly vary from case to case. Of the remaining tasks only laundry and gardening resulted in an increased level of time being allocated by carers who had identified the amount of time spent caring. These both resulted in an increased level of about an hour per week where no other tasks than those specified above were carried out. There was no systematic relationship with frequency of visits. Where these tasks were carried out, therefore, and no time allocated for tasks it was possible to assume an hour was added for each of these tasks per week.

Estimating the cost of time

In accordance with the principles of opportunity costing it is desirable as far as possible to ascertain what would have been done with the time in the absence of disability. A basic assumption in economic theory is that people allocate their time in order to get as much benefit as they can. This is clearly restricted by a number of constraints: the length and distribution of hours in the working week, for example, and the need to earn income.

Table 9.2 Types of household activity

I	Market Activity	- e.g. work for pay
II	Leisure-Pleasure Activity	- e.g. home/public entertainment
III	Meeting Physiological Needs	- e.g. sleep, personal care
IV	Productive Non-market Activity	- e.g. housework, gardening

It is helpful at this stage to categorize time spent by members of the household by type of activity. Table 9.2 illustrates a categorisation of time. Ideally the impact of each type of activity foregone would be costed separately but this presents both theoretical and practical problems. At some point it may be possible to establish an appropriate relationship between the market and non-market productive activity and leisure for the purpose of costing leisure-pleasure time. In order to do this, information is needed about the value of leisure time based on the impact its loss has on market and non-market productivity. This might use the concept of 'slack' in the household: it is reasonable to suppose that where there is time which is genuinely 'free' it should be costed as such. An ideal costing is further complicated by the fact that within each type of activity each additional unit of time given up will, from the carer's perspective, be more costly (rising marginal cost). This is because, all things else being equal, people will give up the activities they value least first and most last. It is tempting when costing informal care to put a lid on escalating costs of individuals carrying a very high burden of care by costing additional hours at a lower cost (e.g. Ernst and Young 1993) but this runs counter to economic theory. These additional hours, perhaps resulting in lost sleep should be costed at a higher rate than the first few hours of care provided. It is unlikely that this could be accurately reflected in any costing in the foreseeable future but a differential costing of types of activity foregone could provide some proxy for this effect.

An issue that also needs to be addressed is the potential for gender bias when costing the care provided within long standing households whose members will have organised household tasks between them prior to the advent of disability. If, for example, an individual ceases to be able to produce meals, but never did so before the advent of disability, there will be no cost. If, however, the household member who produced meals becomes disabled the other member will have to substitute so there will be a cost. Given the predominant way in which household tasks are divided, women with disabilities are likely to be estimated as incurring higher costs to the informal sector than men, and male carers estimated as incurring higher opportunity costs. One way to address this problem is to regard tasks undertaken by household members for the benefit of all household members as outside the scope of costing informal care, and only include specific care such as personal care tasks and monitoring.

There is an extensive economic literature concerned with the valuation and allocation of time between different activities, particularly with reference to the use of different means of transport. The focus of most empirical work, however, is the impact of choices made on the productivity of the market sector. All non-market activity is classified as leisure. Sharp (1981) reviews the literature and describes a model of time allocation which draws on the concepts of productivity of both waged and unwaged time in terms of direct and indirect utility. Wright (1991) examines economic theory from the perspective of valuing the contribution of the informal sector.

There are no clear cut ways of addressing the problem. Extensive theoretically based research is needed before any sophisticated estimation can be attempted. Here a very pragmatic approach is taken. This is based on the fact that while it is often difficult to identify precisely how time would have been spent in the absence of disability, people are usually clear about whether waged or unwaged time has been given up.

Unwaged time

Costing unwaged time is an area of considerable debate and a central issue when considering the contribution of the informal sector. Frequently, carers of elderly people are elderly themselves (Arber and Ginn 1990) and the main bulk of the opportunity cost is in the form of unwaged time.

Wright (1991) suggests an approach to costing time spent on informal care that draws on the concepts of direct and indirect utility. He proposes a weighting based on direct utility associated with caring tasks so the costs incurred from coping with incontinence would receive a higher weighting than those resulting from helping someone to get dressed. This approach attempts to combine the direct and indirect utility effects of caring. Other observers (e.g. Ernst and Young 1993, Nuttall *et al.* 1993) have used the cost of paid carers to provide an estimate of the value (not cost) of the number of hours of care provided by informal carers. The ambition here is more limited – it seeks to assess simply what has been given up in order to care. Feelings about the caring role and what is involved are seen as more appropriately reflected in such scores as Malaise (Rutter *et al.* 1970) or General Health Questionnaire (Goldberg 1972).

In the approach described here, therefore, estimating the opportunity cost of unwaged time requires an estimate of the indirect utility that has been foregone from productive non-market activity. The bulk of productive activity that is common to households and for which there is an assessment of indirect utility is housework. The value that society puts on the indirect utility of these activities is the market wage rate: the hourly rate for domestic help.

It is not suggested that this is ideal: clearly in many cases only leisure time will have been foregone which may feed indirectly if at all into the productivity of the household. Motivations about the caring activity will vary between individuals but in costing it is necessary to assume that the underlying motive is a sense of duty or obligation. Whether the carer enjoys the process of providing care is not the issue; it is something that has got to be done because of the disability and therefore will incur a cost in the sense of lost opportunities. The decision to provide informal care is not the same as that of volunteer activity where it is reasonable to assume an underlying motive which is related to the preferred way of spending time.

Waged time

Informal care commitments can result in considerable reductions in earnings. Changed working patterns and the subsequent loss of income is one of the principal ways in which savings from initiatives to reduce institutionally based care result in increased costs in the informal sector (Muurinen 1986).

Before assessing the opportunity cost of time which would have been spent in waged work, therefore, it is important to be clear about the impact of care responsibilities on participation in waged work. Sometimes a few hours have been taken off from work on an irregular basis, in other circumstances the regular hours of work will be adjusted and the carer will become part-time. In other cases a carer may give up waged work entirely. All the waged time that has been given up because of care should be costed even if it is not spent on caring.

The indirect utility of waged time is clearly the wage rate. If the cost to the carer is to be estimated it is the lost wages, less tax and national insurance, that constitute the opportunity cost. If the time off work has not resulted in lost pay, however, the employer has borne the cost and there is no cost to the carer in indirect utility terms. Work absences may result in long-term career effects, however, which are discussed below.

Major re-adjustments of employment patterns may be made because of caring commitments. If a carer changes to part-time work the expected rate of pay per hour is less than for full time work so the expected wage rate must be distinguished from the actual wage rate. In more extreme cases a carer will give up waged work entirely and the cost is the full-time expected income. In such a situation carers may be eligible for invalid care allowance and other benefits. These need to be deducted from any estimate of lost wage income.

When the cost to society is estimated, however, the cost is the value of the lost production. This is estimated by the wage rate plus the cost of employing the carer as it is this cost to the employer that will equate to the lost productivity. Allowance is therefore made for national insurance and pension contributions as these form part of the marginal cost of employment. All time that would have been spent in waged work is costed this way whether there are lost wages or not. Allowances and benefits should not be included, however, as they do not represent lost production but transfer payments from one sector of society to another.

In estimating the cost to society the possibility exists that there will be no lost production where the carer's former job is filled by a person who would otherwise be unemployed. In such situations there is a change in non-market production between the carer and formerly unemployed person rather than lost production. One approach to this is to assumes that with a 'natural' rate of employment of some seven to nine per cent, where the carer left the labour force, on average seven to nine per cent of the carer's waged hours would be replaced.

When costing time, therefore, it is important to establish how it would have been spent. If it has resulted in lost income then the net effect of this is the opportunity cost to the carer. The lost production that results is the cost to society. Time that would not have been spent in waged work, whether the carer is waged or not, is costed in terms of lost home production, society's valuation of which is the domestic wage rate.

The constraints of employment practice on individuals' ability to spend their time exactly as they would wish have already been identified.

This also applies to the process of giving up waged time to care. Carers may be forced to give up full-time work and unable or unwilling to find another job which takes up the time which is not spent caring. Thus they have time available for non-market productive activity which they would not have had otherwise. This time available should be counted as a benefit to the carer and to society so the cost of waged time will be reduced by the value of household production or domestic wage rate for those hours not spent caring.

Future costs

Another cost of caring can be an impact on the future income of the carer. The disabilities of the elderly person may make it impossible for the carer to meet a requirement to make a heavier time commitment or to move to another part of the country resulting in missed training or job opportunities. Sometimes a carer will change to a less demanding job or one where the hours are more flexible so they can care. Such decisions will affect future career prospects, redundancy and pension rights.

The indirect utility that is lost is future income for the carer or productivity for society. The cost would therefore be the difference in expected future earnings or unearned income resulting from caring responsibilities discounted back to the present time to give a weekly expected loss.

When estimating the cost to society the lost production estimated as the wage rate plus the costs of employment cover the contributions to pensions and other rights that would have been paid by the carer. The cost to the carer, however, should include discounted future income from pensions in addition to lost future wages.

In empirical work on the cost of child bearing and rearing Heather Joshi (1987) estimates the career costs when a mother has returned to full-time work after a break for childbearing and part-time work, and she has lost all the career chances over that period. Her pay was found to be 14 per cent less than her contemporary who worked over that period (Joshi 1987). In examining the effect she notes the number of women in part-time employment over the age of 54 exceeds those in full-time work. There is a consequent drop in expected wage rate independent of the cohort effect. This could be due in part to the effect of caring responsibilities amongst this age group which makes any estimate of lost expected future income as a result of caring responsibilities for elderly people difficult in practice.

Space and privacy

In most cases where a carer and an elderly disabled person share a household, they have done so for a long time before the advent of any disability. In such a situation the spouse is often the principal carer, or a son or daughter who has never left home. Here there are no accommodation costs because no change has resulted from disability.

However, in some cases the difficulties of looking after an elderly person in their own home, whether because of distance or frequency of demands made upon carers, mean that they and the carer decide to share the same household. This can be under a variety of circumstances, upon which depend the opportunity cost.

If the elderly person moves into a room in the carer's home, the room could have yielded the carer indirect utility in the form of rent and this is the appropriate method of costing. The capital value of the house does not enter into the costs because the carer would have been living there in the absence of the elderly person's disability.

Arrangements can be much more complicated than this involving transfers of ownership or future expectations in terms of renting or owning property. Where the costs will lie, in the case of building a granny flat for example, would depend on who made the initial investment and expected distribution of the estate, amongst other things.

In some cases the carer will have moved and in others both the carer and the elderly person moved. When the elderly person is the sole owner or the tenant of the property the carer could be represented as having given up a great deal more than a room's value in terms of space and privacy. However, it is likely that there would, in such cases, be expectations in terms of the future ownership or tenancy and this was the reason that the arrangement had been made. In any costing exercise it is necessary to establish just what these future expectations or specific agreements are before estimating the true opportunity cost.

It is possible that there may be a net benefit to society as a whole if the altered accommodation arrangements result in a more efficient allocation of housing stock. This would be the case if, for example, the elderly person moved out of a large house, releasing it for the use of a family. It is unlikely that a change in accommodation arrangements would result in a more inefficient use of resources. The effect on society would be the difference between the value released from the elderly person's home and the opportunity cost of occupying space in the carer's home.

Assuming no change in capital value, one way of estimating the effect of the change on society would be the difference in the rents that could have been obtained.

An application

This methodology for costing informal care was applied to information collected about the principal carers of elderly people who were receiving community based services in ten local authorities in the mid 1980s. The definition of principal carer excluded spouses and gave priority where there were problems in definition to those sharing the household with the elderly person. Previous analyses (Davies *et al.* 1990) had identified social and community health service resource flows during the first six months of service receipt. While restrictions on the data collected meant an incomplete picture of the contribution of the informal care sector (there was no detailed information about other informal providers of care), it was possible to estimate the opportunity costs for those people identified as principal carers.

Absence of detailed information resulted in a number of assumptions having to be made. The approach to identifying financial expenditure has been identified above but it did not prove possible to include the costs of household capital goods. When costs to the carer were estimated, however, it was possible to include an indicator of financial transactions between households. For the most part it was possible to estimate the cost of waged and unwaged time, making some adjustments for the time that would have been spent with the elderly person in the absence of disability. It was much more difficult to establish the loss of future expectations and a very crude estimate based on Joshi's (1987) work was included. Where the elderly person had moved in with the carer an allowance for loss of space and privacy was made based on the rent of a single room but there was insufficient information about more complex arrangements. Estimates were made of both the cost to society and the cost to the carer. The limitations on the information available meant that these estimates were very close: the average social opportunity cost of care provided by each carer was only £1 less than the average cost to each carer.

The resulting average social opportunity cost to carers of social services clients was £33 per week at 1985 prices and displayed a very high level of variation, ranging from zero to £197 per week. The average cost of social services provided to clients with carers was under £16 per week.

The assumptions that were required were likely to result in an under-estimate rather than an overestimate of the opportunity cost to the carers. Nevertheless, Diagram 9.1 shows that where carers of elderly people receiving mainstream social services were identified, they were bearing over half the costs of caring. This average picture conceals considerable variation in the proportion of costs borne by carers which were related to the total costs of care. The higher the total level of costs incurred by the carer the higher the proportion of total social, health and informal care costs they were bearing. So, when the carer's costs averaged less than £5 per week they were incurring six per cent of the costs, between £5 and £10 about a third of care costs rising to 80 per cent once carer costs were over £50 each week.

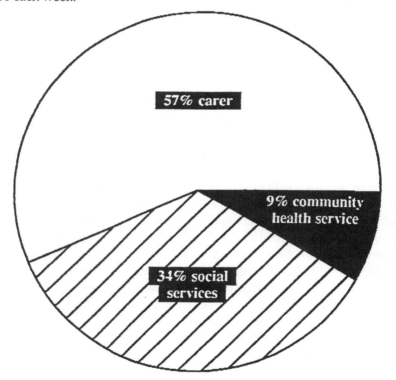

Figure 9.1. Opportunity cost of care for elderly social services clients*
* Clients of social services who identified a carer
Full cost data available for 160 cases

Discussion

Any attempt to provide a detailed opportunity costing requires that assumptions and estimates be made that are open to question. This is especially so in this relatively new area of opportunity costing where conventions have yet to be agreed. In setting out in some detail the methodology used it is hoped that the assumptions are clear so it is possible to assess where and in what directions an estimated cost is likely to vary substantially from the true underlying cost. In the process of estimation two leaps of faith are required: between pure theory and the feasible, and between the feasible and the available.

The dichotomous relationship between statutory agencies and carers (Twigg and Atkin 1993b) means that opportunity cost to carers is both a measure of outcome (when carers are seen as clients) and a measure of input (when they are seen as co-providers). Clearly, therefore, there is considerable potential, once comprehensive costs have been established, to investigate the relationship between costs and key aspects of the supply of informal care and demand for support by carers. These aspects include stress among carers, predictors of breakdown of caring networks, distribution of costs across different types of caring network and effects of service interventions.

Policies for caring cannot reasonably be drawn up with precise accounting information about public sector provision on one hand and ill-defined information about the costs to the informal sector on the other. It is too easy in such circumstances to discount the costs to carers because they are not borne by the public purse. But the demand for personal social services depends as much on the supply of informal care as it does on the prevalence of disability. It is clearly impractical for care managers to estimate the opportunity cost to the caring network when devising a care package within a given budget. Rather, the need is for policies which directly address issues of equity and efficiency in the delivery of care. Such policies could, for example, clarify expectations in terms of the proportion of costs that should be borne by any one individual under different circumstances. Clearer definitions of expectations could then feed into eligibility criteria, the assessment process and needs based planning.

The importance of this policy area is such that the problems associated with estimation should not deter attempts to cost informal care in practice. There is clearly a need for more informed research to improve the balance and the quality of information for policymakers and planners, to facilitate the development of equitable policies towards carer support, and to evaluate the effectiveness of the reforms in improving efficiency in the delivery of care.

Acknowledgements

Much of this chapter is based on 'Costing informal care', in A. Netten and J. Beecham (eds) *Costing Community Care: Theory and Practice.* Aldershot: Ashgate. My thanks are due to Raphael Wittenberg and Karen Traske for their advice on that chapter.

References

Arber, S. and Ginn, J. (1990) 'The meaning of informal care: gender and the contribution of elderly people.' *Ageing and Society 10*, 429–454.

Audit Commission (1986) *Making a Reality of Community Care.* London: HMSO.

Baldwin, S. (1985) *The Costs of Caring.* London: Routledge and Kegan Paul.

Beecham, J. and Netten, A. (eds) (1993) *Community Care in Action: the Role of Costs.* Conference proceedings. Canterbury: Personal Social Services Research Unit, University of Kent at Canterbury.

Caring for People: Community Care in the Next Decade and Beyond (1989). CM 849. London: HMSO.

Challis, D., Chesterman, J. and Traske, K. (1993) 'Case management: Costing the experiments.' In A. Netten and J. Beecham (eds) *Costing Community Care: Theory and Practice.* Aldershot: Ashgate.

Charnley, H. (1989) *Carer Outcomes and the Social Production of Welfare,* Discussion Paper 595. Canterbury: Personal Social Services Research Unit, University of Kent at Canterbury.

Davies, B., Bebbington, A., Baines, B., Charnley, H., Ferlie, E., Hughes, M. and Twigg, J. (1990) *Resources Needs and Outcomes in Community Based Care.* Aldershot: Gower.

Deaton, A.S. and Muellbauer, J. (1980) 'A simple test for heteroscedasticity and random coefficient variation.' *Econometrica 47*, 1287–1294.

Ernst and Young (1993) *The Cost of Maintaining an Elderly Person at Home.* Report to the Department of the Environment.

Finch, J. and Groves, D. (1983) *A Labour of Love: Women, Work and Caring.* London: Routledge and Kegan Paul.

Goldberg, D. (1972) *The Detection of Psychiatric Illness by Questionnaire.* Oxford: Oxford University Press.

Jones, A. and O'Donnell, O. (1992) *Household Equivalence Scales and the Costs of Disability*. Manchester: Department of Econometrics, University of Manchester.

Joshi, H. (1987) *The Cash opportunity Costs of Childbearing: An approach to Estimation using British Data*, Discussion Paper 208. London: Centre for Economic Policy Research.

Levin, E., Sinclair, I. and Gorbach, P. (1989) *Families, Services and Confusion in Old Age*. Aldershot: Avebury.

Muurinen, J.-M. (1986) 'The economics of informal care: Labor market effects in the National Hospice Study.' *Medical Care 24*, 11, 1007–1016.

Netten, A. (1993) 'An economic approach to the social care of elderly people: A perspective on informal care.' In J. Twigg (ed) *Informal Care in Europe*. Proceedings of a conference held in York. York: Social Policy Research Unit, University of York.

Netten, A. and Davies, B. (1990) 'The social production of welfare and consumption of social services.' *Journal of Public Policy 10*, 3, 331–347.

Nuttall, S., Blackwood, R., Bussell, B., Cliff, J., Cornall, M., Cowley, A., Gatenby, P., Webber, J. (1993) *Financing long term care in Great Britain*. Paper presented to the Institute of Actuaries. Oxford: Alden Press.

Phillipson, C. and Walker, A. (1986) *Ageing and Social Policy*. Aldershot: Gower.

Qureshi, H. and Walker, A. (1989) *The Caring Relationship: Elderly People and their Families*. Basingstoke: Macmillan.

Rutter, M. Tizard, J. and Whitmore, K. (1970) *Education, Health and Behaviour*. London: Longmans.

Sharp, C. (1981) *The Economics of Time*. Oxford: Martin Robertson.

Twigg, J. and Atkin, K. (1993a) 'Factors mediating the relationship between carers and service provision.' In J. Twigg (ed) *Informal Care in Europe, Proceedings of a conference held in York*. York: Social Policy Research Unit, University of York.

Twigg, J. and Atkin, K. (1993b) *Carers Perceived: Policy and Practice in Informal Care*. Buckingham: Open University Press.

Twigg, J., Atkin, K. and Perring, C. (1990) *Carers and Services: A Review of Research*. London: HMSO and Social Policy Research Unit, University of York.

Ungerson, C. (1987) *Policy is Personal: Sex, Gender and Informal Care*. London: Tavistock.

Wright, K. (1991) 'Social care versus care by the community: economics of the informal sector.' In J. Pacolet and C. Wilderom (eds) *The Economics of Care of the Elderly*. Aldershot: Avebury.

Caring, Costs And Values
A Concluding Comment

Chris Clark

The community care legislation passed in 1990, and finally implemented in 1993, brought in radical changes in the responsibilities of local authorities for the care of adults with disabilities. One of the major principles incorporated in the changes was to shift the role of the public authorities away from directly providing traditional services to people in need, and towards a more general responsibility for assessing needs and arranging a range of appropriate services. It was taken as a basic principle that services could as well, or better, be run by voluntary organisations or private sector companies as provided directly by the local authorities themselves. The reforms introduced into social services the doctrine of a purchaser-provider split which had already been adopted in the health service.

In consequence of these changes, local authorities have had to take on unfamiliar responsibilities and their staff have had to invent new ways of working. Although the legislation provides a general framework, and government has been liberal to the point of profligacy with its exhortation and policy guidance, in reality little has prepared managers and service professionals for their new responsibilities. They are having to create new methods and systems on the basis of sketchy knowledge of the newly redefined local needs, and fragmentary understanding of the merits of alternative models of care (or case) management. Frontline staff are being asked to carry out new roles, especially as care managers, for which few have been adequately trained, under the direction of managers who have no directly similar experience of their own to draw upon.

Whatever may be the reservations about the models of care management which lie at the heart of the current policy, it is clear that its fundamental principles are not negotiable in the immediate future. Indeed there is much about them, for example the commitment to needs-led assessment and the active involvement of carers in service provision, over which it is difficult to imagine serious disagreement. The issue is to make care management work properly. In part this depends on a series of technical matters to do with accountability, service structures, models for practice, professional training, and so on. But care management is not limited to the merely technical. It cannot escape concern with social and moral values as well as technical efficiency. It will have to entertain complex, intractable and perennially controversial questions about the locus of responsibility for public social service and the nature of the costs they entail.

Key themes: caring, planning, costing
Dimensions of caring
To speak of caring for someone, or of caring services, may refer to any or all of the following responsibilities. (1) Physical care, or tending, means looking after someone's material and bodily needs – 'taking care of'. (2) Moral or psychological care involves the demonstration of interest, affection, sociability, and the practical affirmation of the person's dignity, individuality and worth – 'caring about'. In ordinary life we commonly expect physical and moral care to go together, and the main arena of their joint expression is the family under the obligations of close kinship. To a considerable extent, caring in the one sense requires the other, and this interdependence is reflected in ordinary language: we care for (in the physical sense) those whom we care about (in the moral sense); we usually care for (in the sense of liking) those for whom we have moral responsibilities. (3) It is also possible to speak of care as a more abstract concern or regard for someone's welfare and interests, which may be exercised impersonally without any direct contact. This is exemplified in the legal 'duty of care', which requires in effect that we should be careful, and not be careless, of someone's interests that have a legitimate call on our attention.

Much ambiguity about caring is submerged in community care policy. The need for some kind of public policy to provide for the physical care of adults with disabilities has of course been accepted for several centuries. It is not that any such policy could be called 'community care', except in the loosest and most general sense. A modern community care policy should adequately recognise the moral dimension of caring; any modern view regards physical tending as merely one component of decent care. Public policy is therefore obliged to tread, however ineptly or clumsily, into the essentially private sphere of 'caring about'. This is the source of the dissonance that so quickly catches the ear in the rhetoric of community care. Public administration can be expected to cope reasonably well with objectively measurable needs and quantifiable practical services. It struggles when expected to exercise a moral authority for which no clear social mandate has been created. Under such circumstances its agents and practitioners will be faced with contradictory demands.

The new legislation imposes particular duties on local authorities. It remains to be seen whether they will be legally challenged if their practice in community care shows insufficient care for the interests of those affected. Litigation has not, in Britain, been a significant avenue for the expression of discontent with public services. The cost and complexity of going to law, and the ambiguity of rights under legislation which largely depends on the exercise of discretionary powers, have been among the factors making it unattractive to do so. If the law does not often appear to provide a practicable remedy, other means will need to be developed. The elements of care may be distinguished conceptually, but the practice of care is indivisible. The community soon smells the irony of community care policy apparently exercised with too little care. The steady development of movements that emphasise the rights of citizens to participate in the control of services reflects more stringent public expectations about quality.

Planning and costing care

On the basis of the government's legislation and detailed guidance, one could be excused for imagining that devising and costing an individual care plan was basically a straightforward matter of applying the assessment schema so ingeniously crafted by central policy experts and then choosing the locally most cost-effective intervention to meet the need revealed. Such assumptions are dangerously simplistic, first because, as we have already seen, care is complex and riddled with ambiguities and conflicts of priority. Second, the assumptions behind the policy of care planning are unsatisfactory because they rest on inadequate analysis of the multiple aspects of assessment and costing.

Part of this problem is technical. As regards frameworks for assessment, comprehensive, dependable and feasible measures do not yet exist for assessing the needs of adults who may need care in the community. As regards costing services, this is still a very tentative business where prices are often merely notional and exact costs almost impossible to measure accurately. Beyond these technical problems, however, lie unresolved theoretical and philosophical issues. Can the costs (and benefits) of caring all be reduced to a single, monetary measure? Is caring not ultimately dictated by social values and obligations not amenable to rationalist planning and cost accountancy? More pragmatically – can welfare professionals reconcile their commitment to clients with their role of regulating public expenditure?

Issues in planning and costing community care
Assessment, needs and costs: service costs don't reflect need satisfaction
Assessment is the linchpin of care management practice. The whole process begins with the initial sorting and grading of applicants' needs. What should emerge from assessment is classification and quantification of need. On the basis of the assessment, entitlement is established to certain services at certain volumes. Appropriate services are then set up, corresponding to the level and nature of need; costs are controlled; and equity is ensured as between different consumers.

Unfortunately for practitioners and agencies, there are many problems with this idealised picture. Assessment of need is a very inexact science, even at a purely qualitative level. Experienced practitioners frequently disagree (on empirical grounds) about whether a particular state of affairs actually amounts to a need serious enough to warrant intervention; and they may disagree about the appropriate remedies. They may also disagree (on theoretical grounds) about the nature of need (do disabled people 'need' a free television licence?).

Where serviceable measures of need can be agreed, there is no easy path from assessed need to amount of service entitlement as measured by service cost. A gross quantification of need does not permit an estimate of the value of the service entitlement, because different clients whose needs are equivalently weighty may need services to satisfy those needs that are not equivalently costly. For example, nursing or personal care is liable to be more costly at awkward times (evenings, weekends) and places (remote rural locations) than the same care at more convenient times and places; or structural modification to a house may cost much more than a dietary supplement. Since it is difficult to quantify overall service entitlement in other than monetary terms, there is a risk that relying on pragmatic measures of costs may lead to inequitable allocation of resources between different users. Estimating social need is ultimately and unavoidably a value judgement in the largest sense.

Prices are a poor guide to care management
The cost of services is, then, wholly inadequate as a measure of their capacity to satisfy needs. A further problem is that for a number of reasons, the price that authorities or individual consumers pay for a service may be a poor reflection of its actual cost. Labour intensive activities such as caring services are very sensitive to rapidly changing efficiency at the margin. For example, an empty day care place results in very little saving in running costs for the centre, so that the average cost of the occupied places rises. Another reason why prices may be a poor reflection of costs is that prices are likely to be standardised in any given service area, disguising cost variations due to such things as local geography or the effectiveness of different staff and their management.

For pricing to be used as a practical regulatory mechanism in the allocation of service, either through actual purchase on a fully commercial basis or as a tool for decision making in a notional internal market, it is clearly necessary to have a system of reasonably stable and consistent pricing which mostly removes contingent and short term variations in cost from the purchaser's view. Thus commercial firms or voluntary organisations enter contracts to provide a unit of service at a certain price, accepting a risk that the resultant income will cover costs (and also show a profit, in the case of private firms). Within public-sector organisations, sets of notional standardised prices can be adopted. While these mechanisms have their uses, there are clearly dangers involved. In the specialised field of community care at the local level, the frequent absence of any potential rival suppliers means little competition and a virtual monopoly. Equally, since the local authority may be practically the only purchaser, there is reduced incentive for other suppliers to look for opportunities. For these and other reasons, the local supply of community care services seldom resembles anything like a genuine market. In the absence of an effective market, prices can drift well apart from costs.

A particularly significant feature of community care is that much of the actual cost of caring falls not on formal organisations but on the close kin of care receivers. Informal care is given and received outwith the mechanisms of the market or the regulation of bureaucracies and is difficult to measure. It is, however, clearly essential to measure the costs of informal care if care management is not to become a mechanism for exploiting the goodwill of families.

We have therefore a twofold problem for care management. Care management entails a purchaser-provider split. The care manager optimises need satisfaction, at any given level of external resources, by purchasing for the client an individualised package of care services. The first problem is that the cost of providing services does not accurately reflect the satisfaction of need. It is unsafe to conclude that, because someone is receiving a substantial amount of help, their need is being significantly reduced. Second, prices are not a very reliable guide to costs. The lack of good information about costs is likely to lead to poor care management choices at the levels both of the individual case and the overall service programme.

Care management and implications for policy

Care management is the central concept in the new community care policy. This reconnaissance suggests that the problems of implementing it are not limited to the sheer labour that is required in any large administrative reorganisation, considerable though it is. Care management depends on theories and methods for assessment, and for costing services, which are still far from adequately workable in many areas of need and service. Like most major reorganisations in the social services, the community care reforms are to a great extent a leap in the dark, driven by a combination of ideology, necessity and expediency. Inevitably, practitioners and managers will stumble as they try to find their way over unfamiliar territory, bidden by a political imperative, and equipped with only a fragmentary sketch map of dubious accuracy.

How the shortcomings of the model of care management seriously put at risk the aims of the policy, will be better revealed as experience unfolds. For example, there is already abundant anecdote to the effect that needs-led assessment, icon of the new approach, has not in fact generally superseded old-fashioned assessment for available service. Needs-led assessment has an imaginary quality in a world where priorities must be to find answers to today's problems with today's inadequate systems and resources.

Value conflicts? The unmeasurable value of caring

It is not only organisational and technical difficulties which threaten to undermine community care policy built on the foundation of care management. The model of care management requires the benefits and costs of different courses of action to be estimated, both in individual cases and as global aggregates, in order to decide upon particular interventions and to plan agency programmes. This approach, given the necessary research and development, potentially offers a method for planning physical care. It is not, however, likely to be adequate for measuring the moral and psychological aspects of caring.

Caring in the latter senses is not measurable in terms of the prices used to cost packages of care. The respect which should be shown towards all persons, including those with dependencies; the affection in which they are held and the honour shown; the status they are accorded, are literally priceless. Without these qualities, the caring process has very little point; nobody should be satisfied with caring as the purely mechanical tending of physical needs. The different aspects of caring remain inseparable in the practice of caring.

The issue here is that the values and costs of care in the physical sense seem to be incommensurable with the values and costs of caring in the moral and psychological senses. This raises a fundamental problem for care management. If there is no satisfactory method of weighing both the physical, and the moral and psychological, aspects of care in the same scales, the obvious danger is that methods will be adopted that seem efficiently to account for the physical needs but overlook the more intangible aspects. Examples of this problem in practice are easy to find. People value the care they receive not only for its instrumental value but also for the moral and affective relationship that it affirms. It is not the same to have one's housework done by an efficient paid stranger as it is to have it done by the dependable welfare employee who has, over years, grown into a friend. It is not the same to be helped by a paid employee as it is to be helped by a spouse, a son or a daughter.

It is tempting, though probably incorrect, to view these rival perspectives as the properties and traditions of the different professions involved. The so-called caring professions are quick to assert the social and moral values that supposedly inform their practice. Their warm, humanistic theory is readily contrasted with the cold, impersonal calculations of cost accountants who would not venture to make valuations of the ineffable. A reading of the research on social workers and their practice demands a much more temperate interpretation. Social workers seem no more immune than any other comparable group to falling in with routinised, bureaucratically-oriented practices which do scant justice to the infinite colours of human need. Equally, no manager can permanently enforce rationalistic systems of cost control which go against the grain of community and political preference.

Whatever may be the orientations of the various actors and occupational groups involved in community care, it is clear that there is scope indeed for multiple conflicts of values: not only in the restricted sense of cost accountancy, but also as normative moral and political principles. Those involved in the design and delivery of community care services must aim to build conceptual bridges between the worlds of management accounting and personal caring if they are to reconcile the equally indispensable and pressing demands of public policy and decent care for individuals.

The Contributors

Laura Bannerman is Principal Officer Community Care Planning, Social Work Department, Tayside Regional Council.

Lorna Cameron is Senior Research Officer, Social Work Department, Strathclyde Regional Council.

Chris Clark is Senior Lecturer in Social Work at the University of Edinburgh.

Isobel Freeman is Principal Officer, Information and Research, Social Work Department, Strathclyde Regional Council.

Margaret King is Lecturer in Accounting and Associate Research Fellow of the Institute of Public Sector Accounting Research, University of Edinburgh.

Irvine Lapsley is Professor of Accounting and Director of the Institute of Public Sector Accounting Research, University of Edinburgh.

Sue Llewellyn is Senior Lecturer in Accounting and Depute Director of the Institute of Public Sector Accounting Research, University of Edinburgh.

Stephen Maxwell is Assistant Director, Scottish Council for Voluntary Organisations, and Honorary Fellow, Department of Social Policy, University of Edinburgh.

Terry McLean is Senior Lecturer in Social Work, Robert Gordon University, Aberdeen.

Ann Netten is Research Fellow, Personal Social Services Research Unit, University of Kent at Canterbury.

Alison Petch is Professor, Nuffield Centre for Community Care Studies, University of Glasgow.

Bill Robertson is Depute Director, Social Work Department, Tayside Regional Council.

Phyllis Sturges is Associate Professor, College of Social Work, San Jose State University, California. At the time of writing of the chapter for this book she was a visiting scholar in the Department of Social Work, University of Dundee.

Mike Titterton is an Edinburgh-based independent consultant, specialising in training and research.